# WINGS OF THE DESERT

*From Emirates to SpaceX Crew*



## MATTHEW COCHRAN

*To my children, whose laughter is my favorite sound.*

*"Meanwhile, I cannot refrain from contributing this additional feature to the unorthodox aspects of your findings. It is not improbable, I must point out, that there are inhabitants not only on the moon but on Jupiter too or (as was delightfully remarked at a recent gathering of certain philosophers) that those areas are now being unveiled for the first time. But as soon as somebody demonstrates the art of flying, settlers from our species of man will not be lacking. Who would once have thought that the crossing of the wide ocean was calmer and safer than of the narrow Adriatic Sea, Baltic Sea, or English Channel? Given ships or sails adapted to the breezes of heaven, there will be those who will not shrink from even that vast expanse. Therefore, for the sake of those who, as it were, will presently be on hand to attempt this voyage, let us establish the astronomy, Galileo, you of Jupiter, and me of the moon."*

-In 1610, Johannes Kepler, the distinguished astronomer, corresponded with Galileo Galilei in response to Galilei's book from the same year.

Kepler's letter discussed various astronomical discoveries and their implications, contributing to the advancement of scientific knowledge during that era.

# Table of Contents

# INTRODUCTION

The United Arab Emirates has now established itself as a global player in the aviation and space industry. The country's long journey, based upon an old affinity with the stars, began in 1985 when the UAE took its first foray into aviation, setting up Emirates Airlines with leased planes. Now in 2023, the world has witnessed the UAE take a leadership role with the success of Dr. Sultan Al Neyadi returning to Earth and celebrated by his country and the world as having achieved what was planned by the wise leadership of the UAE.

The country has invested heavily in aerospace and infrastructure, seeing it as a way to diversify the economy and transform the UAE into a high-technology hub. Gradually, the nation's leaders laid the foundations, carefully investing for the future with long-term aims and clarity about exactly what they wanted to achieve.

Looking to the future, the country has already sent a successful probe to Mars and wants to set up a base on the planet for human exploration within a century. Patiently, the UAE is helping dreams and visions become reality, with the space program becoming a source of national pride and a cornerstone of the country's technological transformation.

In this book, we will explore the history of the UAE's aviation and space journey. By charting progress from the early days of Emirates Airlines to the country's latest achievements and future goals, we show how some of these leadership skills can inspire your business aims and even everyday life goals.

## A Beginning

The Arab world has a long history of watching the skies, with navigators and scholars plotting and predicting the movements of stars, contributing their wisdom to human knowledge. For millennia, the clear skies and stars over the Arabian Peninsula helped travelers and traders navigate the trackless deserts. Knowing the constellations and the directions hidden in the sky often meant the difference between life and death.

This long tradition of *anwā'* on the Arabian Peninsula, stretching back deep into Bedouin history, mapped 28 stars and constellations to provide a calendar and gave Arabs their rich tradition of astronomy. They used the stars as a guide of when to plant crops, and the culture developed rich poetry, stories, proverbs, and knowledge. Islamic scholars collected this body of knowledge, condensing it and writing it down in the *Kutub al-anwā'*, the books of the *anwā'*

The Arabs understood the sky and its importance, and this familiarity never really left them, remaining as a tradition still shaping their culture until the present day. This attachment to the firmament now manifests as an interest in space programs that draw upon the long tradition of Arab explorers and scholars. In the Arab world, space expeditions still create excitement and the UAE is no different, finding no shortage of young Emiratis keen to contribute.

In many ways, Emiratis are reconnecting with the old affinity with the heavens and astronomy ingrained deep in their history. Even now, young Emiratis quote the old *anwā'* proverbs they grew up with that stretch back millennia. The UAE's space program truly inspires them and shows how the past can inspire the future.

Naturally, alongside romanticism, the UAE has many practical reasons for developing a space program steeped in the complex politics of the Middle East and the difficulty of shifting the economy away from oil and gas wealth.

## Politics and Public Relations

Of course, while the UAE's space program is built upon a long history, nostalgia isn't the only reason that the UAE is investing resources. In one way, space is like Antarctica or the deepest oceans, where humans work together for a common cause. Away from borders and politics, scientists, engineers, and astronauts work together and share information and research. Perhaps, when surrounded by boundless space and looking back on Earth, divides disappear, and Carl Sagan's words about the pale blue dot ring true.

On the other side, rivalries and jostling for regional influence also play a role and the UAE's successful missions to Mars alongside sending astronauts to the ISS have created a regional space race as its neighbors strive to catch up. These regional rivalries mean that the UAE, Egypt, Saudi Arabia, and other countries in the region invest in space exploration and are making the region into an international hub. This competition fuels innovation and encourages investment and developing resources and infrastructure.

Of course, while rivals, the countries also collaborate and share knowledge, developing hi-tech aerospace industries across the Middle East. These entice foreign companies, organizations, and scientists to work in the area and create a dynamic and interlinked ecosystem that brings together some of the best minds in the world. For the UAE, this means an exciting future and a way for the country to thrive and build for the benefit of generations of Emiratis.

For the UAE, the space program sprang from a dream that started to bloom when the US astronauts first landed on the moon, with the entire world watching this monumental moment in history. The dream led to a plan, which started with Emirates Airlines and patiently building an aerospace industry from scratch. From two leased aircraft, the UAE followed a path toward building satellites and contributing to high profile international space missions.

# CHAPTER 1

## THE BIRTH OF EMIRATES AIRLINES

In the UAE, it is impossible to discuss its space program without looking at the history of Emirates Airlines and its astonishing growth over four decades. This company and the associated infrastructure are inseparable from the space program because it helped the country take its first steps. As its aviation industry grew, the UAE developed aerospace infrastructure, attracted specialist knowledge, and inspired the first generation of Emirati engineers, scientists, and technicians.

The UAE has a historical affinity with outer space. Long ago, its people developed their knowledge of astronomy, navigating by the stars to travel by land and sea. The founder of the United Arab Emirates, the late Sheikh Zayed bin Sultan Al Nahyan, drew on this deep tradition. As a visionary with ambitions of helping his country explore space, he welcomed a NASA delegation as early as 1976.[1]

This initial fascination with space developed into a program using the money from the nation's oil wealth, providing a catalyst for far-sighted leaders to begin building an entire industry from nothing. The first steps that brought the vision into a tangible process began a decade later.

---

[1] www.space.gov.ae/Documents/PublicationPDFFiles/Introduction%20to%20UAE%E2%80%99s%20National%20Space%20Policy.pdf

In 1985, Sheikh Ahmed bin Saeed Al Maktoum founded Emirates Airlines with just two aircraft, seeking to tap into the growing aviation market. From the very beginning, the aim was to create a world-class airline for the UAE, connecting the country with the rest of the world.

Today, Emirates is one of the world's leading airlines, operating over 3,600 flights a week to more than 144 destinations worldwide. Through every part of the airline's journey, the UAE has supported growth with a plethora of infrastructure programs and encouraging education to give its workforce the necessary skills.

Now, Emirates Airlines is part of the UAE's national identity and a success story that few other airlines can match. The company provides an example of how having a vision helps to put in place a plan and develop a framework for getting there.

## The Origins of Emirates

Although the company soon became one of the most recognized airlines in the world, Emirates Airlines originally emerged from necessity. The country needed to develop its own airline if it was to remain connected to the wider world and undergo the program of modernization developed by the country's leaders.

Before Emirates, Bahrain's Gulf Air served the UAE with a number of flights, but started to cut back its services in the mid-1980s. With no air service, the UAE risked isolation and it would become difficult to attract investment, build tourism, or help the country become outward looking. At a time when the world was starting to become interconnected, isolation was simply not an option.

The 1980s became a time of technological evolution when the world was advancing rapidly, and the UAE's Royal Family realized that Gulf Air's withdrawal could strike a fatal blow to their ambitions for modernizing the country and using its oil wealth funds to build for the future.

In response, the UAE decided to set up its own airline and Emirates Airlines emerged from a humble start belying the global aviation behemoth it would eventually become. However, as always, their ambitions stretched beyond their immediate needs and they began to put the right people and processes in place to build an airline that would serve Emiratis for decades.

## The Idea is Born

In 1984 Sheikh Mohammed bin Rashid al Maktoum looked into setting up a national airline. To make sure that the airline could get off to a good start, get the basics right, and immediately impact the market, the UAE searched the globe for the right people, bringing in Maurice Flanagan, with a wealth of experience from the Dubai National Air Travel Agency (DNATA) and British Airways to act as CEO.

All across its plan to develop a modern, technological economy, this idea of finding the right people has been a recurring theme for the UAE. Later, in 2003, they hired Tim Clark, with a background in aviation, to be the Head of Airline Planning.

With an experienced veteran in charge, Sheikh Mohammed believed that the UAE would be able to set up the airline and start delivering profits quickly. Flanagan found himself faced with a mission that was challenging even for a veteran of the industry, and he had to find a way to set up an airline in an extremely short timescale of five months. Sheikh Mohammed wanted an airline set up in just five months, but he also had a vision for an airline that would "look good, be good, and make money."

Adding to the difficulty, Flanagan had only $10 million seed funding, no further subsidies, and the challenge of an open skies policy which meant the company would have no protection from competition. Undaunted, Flanagan got to work in March and, by December, the business plan was ready and the name chosen. Emirates Airlines was ready to take its first steps and underpin the development of the UAE's domestic aviation industry.[2]

## The Need for Support

Initially, because the newly-named airline did not have the financial means to buy its own aircraft, Flanagan sought support from Pakistan International Airlines. As part of the agreement, Emirates received technical support, and administrative help, and opted to lease two aircraft from Pakistan International Airlines. Although Emirates aircraft, the airline used PIA pilots initially until it could train Emirati pilots and crew.[3]

---

[2] https://www.emirates.com/english/about-us/timeline
[3] Hayward, J., The Rise Of Emirates: A PIA Investment To Global Mega Airline, *Simple Flying*, December 3, 2020, https://simpleflying.com/rise-of-emirates/?newsletter_popup=1

The airline also used two Boeing 727-200 aircraft loaned by the royal family's Dubai Air Wing. These aircraft possessed greater range and more powerful engines, increasing the airline's options for new routes, and these aircraft worked with Emirates for ten years.[4]

On October 25, 1985, Emirates operated its first flights from Dubai to Mumbai and Karachi with a Boeing 737 and a leased Airbus 300 B4, marking the start of Emirate Airlines' illustrious rise.[5] Later on, in 2023, the UAE and Pakistan International Airlines would continue this relationship when Pakistan offered wealth funds in the UAE the opportunity to invest in Pakistani airlines and airports.

In its first year, Emirates transported around 260,000 passengers and 10,000 tons of freight, capturing market share from Gulf Air, whose profits dropped by over half in Emirate Airline's first year of operation. The next year, Gulf Air actually reported a loss while its Emirati counterpart continued to thrive. Soon, Emirates Airlines took on more routes, now covering destinations including Delhi, Colombo, Cairo, and Dhaka.[6] Aggressive marketing and careful selection of routes soon helped the new airline forge a strong reputation in the Gulf region.[7]

In 1986, the airline added a number of routes, including Colombo and Cairo, and started to add new aircraft to its roster in the next few years. On July 3, 1987, Emirates purchased its own

---

[4] Hayward, 2020

[5] https://www.emirates.com/english/about-us/timeline

[6] Kylie, N., Starting Off Small: The Story of Emirate's Foundation, *Simple Flying*, March 25, 2023, https://simpleflying.com/emirates-foundation-story/

[7] Hayward, 2020

aircraft, including an Airbus A310-304, and soon opened new routes covering Male, Frankfurt, Istanbul, and Kuwait. [8]

Within a very short time, of less than five years, the airline flew to 14 destinations and recorded an average annual growth of over 30% in its first decade. Clearly, Emirates Airlines was here to stay and was now disrupting Middle Eastern markets, challenging the incumbents but also taking the first steps to establishing the UAE as a regional aviation hub.

Aware of fierce competition in the region, Emirates explored a number of ways to distinguish itself from its competitors. From the start, the airline leaned heavily on luxury and business class, creating a strong corporate message alongside a willingness to install new passenger-friendly technologies such as entertainment systems for every seat, real-time communication services, and many other novel ideas that would become standard across most airlines.

Emirates Airlines' willingness to become a first-adopter of new technologies and focus on the passenger service is a philosophy now engrained in its approach and continuing to this day.

## The Importance of Vision and Long-Term Goals

Many advances in business, technology, and even your own personal life often emerge from adversity and the need to solve a problem quickly. The withdrawal of Gulf Air was a huge problem for the UAE and its leaders needed to find a solution. Importantly,

---

[8] Kylie, 2023

although they set up their new airline quickly, this was never going to be a short-term fix.

Even at this stage, the UAE's leaders looked to the longer term, seeing the new airline as an integral component of their strategy to modernize the country. A thriving aviation industry would act as a focus for developing a knowledge base, a reputation, and a sector where public organizations and the private sector worked closely together, bringing in expertise and targeting investments to help businesses develop to serve the new airline.

The airline also showed the UAE's willingness to import expertise where needed, something it does across many industries. Hiring experienced executives made sure that the new airline could thrive, and the right people in the right places helped to drive the vision forward, knowing what to do and when to do it.

Of course, the UAE's leaders also understand that this only ever forms part of the vision and, while seeking expertise is part of that, eventually, the country needs to make sure that it starts to produce its own experience and skilled people, also investing in knowledge and education alongside the physical infrastructure. This became apparent when the airline had to lease crew from PIA, and training Emirati crew became a priority for the government.

Education and planning infrastructure are both long term goals that take years to start contributing, and as visions translate into plans, need to be taken into account. Understanding the skills your present staff need is crucial, but thinking ahead and looking at what skills future staff will need to cope with new technologies and challenges is also important.

Emirates Airlines, from its initial plan, had a vision of where it wanted to go and how it could distinguish itself from competitors. Focusing on the corporate market, long hauls, and prioritizing customers became hallmarks of the airline that would actually underpin growth.

Importantly, as soon as they leased the first two aircraft, the UAE understood that it needed infrastructure because just buying aircraft was not enough. They needed airports, roads, fuel, logistics, maintenance facilities and all the other infrastructure that an airline needs.

# CHAPTER 2

## BUILDING THE INFRASTRUCTURE

In the previous chapter, we saw how the UAE set up Emirates airline in response to Gulf Air cutting flights. By finding the right people to set up the company, it soon grew to become one of the dominant airlines in the region. However, for the UAE, this was only part of the equation, and realizing its ambition of becoming a regional and even global hub for aviation and aerospace needed infrastructure and services to support aircraft.

To handle the increasing number of aircraft and passengers, the UAE invested heavily in building infrastructure, including airports, air traffic control systems, and aviation training facilities.

For a country built on oil and gas and with many sovereign investment funds, investing in infrastructure became crucial for developing and future -proofing the economy. The government took a proactive approach towards infrastructure, understanding that it needed to invest in airports and air traffic control. However, it also needed to invest in all of the other services that support the aviation industry, and promote international collaboration to help develop expertise.

Naturally, with Emirates and other airlines like Etihad growing, the UAE had to invest in airports to cope with higher volumes of aircraft and passengers, and longer runways to handle bigger, heavier planes. Once again, the country's leaders understood the need to think ahead, given the long lead times for building airports and the associated infrastructure.

## Airports

The UAE has seven international airports including Dubai International Airport and Abu Dhabi International Airport. In recent decades, the UAE government invested heavily in airport development and expansion projects. These include $8.1 billion spent on the Al Maktoum International Airport in Dubai and $7.6 billion for the Dubai International Airport Expansion Phase 4.

Emirates airline uses Dubai International Airport's Terminal 3, built for its exclusive use at a cost of $4.5 billion and opened in 2008. This modern terminal is the second largest building in the world with respect to floor space. It can handle 43 million passengers per year and a new Concourse C, in 2013, opened for use with the A380-800.

## Developing Al Maktoum International Airport

As Emirates and other airlines expanded, along with growing tourism in the UAE and an increase in air freight, the UAE began developing new facilities with an eye on the future. This resulted in long term plans to build the Al Maktoum International Airport, which would be surrounded by all the services and support it needs.

The airport, to be finished in 2027, first opened in 2010 and is part of a growing logistics, commercial, and residential project. It will include servicing, logistics, manufacturing, and an economic free zone to encourage inward investment and take advantage of the air services, especially freight. It will become part of Dubai World

Central and one of the largest airports in the world, helping Dubai fulfil its goal of becoming a major international air hub.

Supporting infrastructure will include parking, a hyperloop to connect to Dubai International Airport, high speed rail, and the Dubai Metro.

This particular project shows how the UAE sees aviation and airports as a part of its economic diversification and how they will offer support to other industries and sectors. Infrastructure isn't just about airports and planes but about the surrounding industries, businesses, and economic environments needed to create a strong aerospace industry that will thrive long into the future.

## Government Initiatives and Investments

The UAE government has invested heavily in aerospace, using offsets, strategic investments, setting up industrial clusters, and creating links with universities and researchers. These investments always have the future in mind and look at training Emiratis, supporting local businesses, and building a knowledge economy alongside creating hard infrastructure like airports and bridges.

## The UAE's Aerospace Companies

The EDGE Group and Mubadala are heavily involved in aerospace, creating partnerships with Boeing, Airbus, Lockheed Martin, BAE Systems, Northrop Grumman, Rolls-Royce, the National Aeronautics and Space Administration (NASA), and Piaggio Aerospace. The two organizations work closely together within the framework of economic diversification and upskilling.

Mubadala develops maintenance facilities for civil and commercial aircraft, flight training, logistics and parts, and R&D. Other companies operating under the Mubadala group's umbrella all play a role in supporting the UAE's growing aerospace sector. Each of these companies contributes to the physical and intangible infrastructure needed to support the UAE's plan to develop its aerospace industry.

## Manufacturing

The Mubadala Aerospace subsidiary is responsible for developing maintenance facilities for commercial aircraft, alongside manufacturing parts, research and development, and flight training.

As part of Mubadala's remit of promoting collaboration, Strata Manufacturing develops partnerships with aerospace companies across the world. This helps the UAE access the latest technology and training, and incorporate the most efficient manufacturing practices. Some of the companies the company has worked with include EADS /Airbus, SABCA, FACC, and Finmeccanica/AleniaAeronautica.

Strata supplies a number of components to Boeing, including ribs for the 777, vertical fin ribs for the 787 Dreamliner, and composite ribs for the 777X.

## Maintenance

The UAE is setting itself up as a regional hub for Maintenance, Repair, and Overhaul (MRO), and already has at least 46 MRO companies registered with the GCAA. This ensures that the country has ample MRO capacity for its own fleets but has room to expand and offer services to carriers from other nations.

One way to build the UAE's aircraft maintenance capacity is with an engineering center located at Dubai International Airport. It employs 5,550 people, including over 1,000 engineers to check, maintain, and repair aircraft. [9]

Moving to individual companies, Sanad Aerotech and Turbine Services & Solutions, a subsidiary of Mubadala, Sanad provides maintenance, repair, and overhaul (MRO) for a wide range of aircraft. These include Boeing's 747 and 787, and Airbus' A300, A320, and A330. Sanad has a number of partnerships with manufacturers and service providers including Rolls Royce, Siemens, and GE.

Working with Emirates Engineering, GE Aviation operates a support center that provides maintenance and repair for GE and CFM engines. In another example of working with partners, Emirates Engineering sought the help of Engine Alliance, a GE and P&W company, to service and repair 90 GP7200 Airbus A380 engines for the Emirates fleet.

## Training

To supply the skilled personnel needed for maintenance, manufacturing, and the countless other jobs needed within the aviation industry, the UAE emphasizes training.

---

[9] Kamarudeen, Niyazudeen and Sundarakani, Balan, Business And Supply Chain Strategy Of Flying Above The Desert: A Case Study Of Emirates Airline, *9th International Conference on Operations and Supply Chain Management, Vietnam*, 2019,

The UAE will require at least 22,000 pilots and aircrew by 2033, so has already invested in training facilities. It is also investing heavily in modern flight simulators and developing skilled staff for all parts of the aviation industry, including technicians, mechanics, IT specialists, air traffic controllers, and all the other people it will need. Adopting a best-in-class approach will also enhance the reputation of training in the UAE and attract students from the MENA region and even further afield

Emirates airline understands the importance of training and invested heavily in facilities and hiring highly experienced trainers for pilots, technicians, control staff, and all the other necessary people needed to make an airline work. This is a philosophy that the UAE later extended into its space program, building upon existing systems and knowledge base.

Some of the notable programs the UAE set up for its aviation industry include a number of well-funded training institutes. The Emirates Aviation University provides education and training for the aviation industry, including aerospace engineers and technicians.

To provide comprehensive experience, the Emirates Flight Training Academy collaborates with Boeing for training materials and software.[10] Its facilities include flight simulators, an airport, air traffic control tower, and emergency services to best emulate real conditions.

Emirates CAE Flight Training, a joint venture between Emirates and CAE of Canada, trains flight deck crew and also maintenance

---

[10] Kamarudeen and Sundarakani, 2019

personnel. It includes flight simulators for a number of fixed wing aircraft and helicopters at its two facilities in Dubai.[11]

## Airport Services

To serve its airports, the UAE provides a number of supplementary services to make sure that everything runs smoothly. These help Emirates keep its reputation as a very high-quality provider and support the country's other carriers in building up a successful aviation industry. These include ground services, logistics, and all of the other airport services needed.

In any airport, although it is very easy to focus on aircraft and engineering, it is the thousands of ground support services that make everything work. People flying long haul are not worried about the technical specifications of the engine. What they want is to check in quickly and have a comfortable flight with good catering.

In the UAE, airports partner with a number of specialist companies to oversee the many jobs that keep airports moving. Hospitality, catering, baggage handling, and duty free are all taken care of to a high level of service, and the country's airports constantly look to refine and improve.

Moving people is only one part of work in an airport, and Dubai National Air Travel Agency (DNATA), part of the Emirates group, is responsible for cargo services and ground handling.

---

[11] https://www.cae.com/civil-aviation/aviation-services/partners/emirates-cae-flight-training/

Aware that there are always ways to improve processes and enhance the customer experience, the in-house R&D Center of Emirates looks for continuous improvement in existing technologies and products. It seeks to maximize efficiency, covering everything from passenger experience to maintenance and baggage handling. [12]

Aware that it will expand its fleet in the future, the UAE is already investing in the infrastructure needed, with a raft of planned airport expansions and new hangars. The country is not afraid to make targeted investments in developing airport infrastructure.

## Be Proactive and Build the Foundations with the End in Mind

In a relatively short time, the UAE has invested vast resources in improving its physical infrastructure to make its airports bigger and more able to cope with increased traffic. However, the country targeted its investments well, starting with goals and a firm idea of where it wanted to be before working out the different elements it needed to get there. The UAE's planning saw it becoming a regional hub for aviation services and many of the programs it developed as it followed its plan had that end goal in sight.

Behind the scenes, the UAE developed all the many services it needed to support its aviation industry, from maintenance and repair to the ancillary services needed to enhance the passenger experience and keep airports running. Bringing services under the remit of the EDGE and Mubadala Investment groups promotes synergy and ensures that there are no gaps in the program.

---

[12] Kamarudeen and Sundarakani, 2019

In addition, EDGE and Mubadala are well practiced at building partnerships with others, and if they feel that they need expertise, will find partners to provide the knowledge and technology they need. This is a philosophy the UAE follows for other sectors, such as oil and gas and military equipment, so it is a well-tested and trusted path. As the aviation program started to germinate the space program, it is important to note that EDGE and Mubadala continued this practice.

Notably, the UAE's leaders did not set out with the goal of simply providing the services needed to run its own services and fleets. The country built in extra capacity at every stage with the awareness that it wants to become a regional hub for aviation whether maintenance or baggage handling.

It also adopts an approach that very much focuses on quality, partly because Emirates Airline's growth is underpinned by its very high standards and partly because, in an industry with fine margins and where errors simply cannot happen, reputation is everything.

For example, if the UAE's MRO centers show that they are excellent and offer excellent service, then other carriers are more likely to trust them and start using them. Accordingly, high standards define every stage of the UAE's aviation program and are hardwired into its planning.

Because of the long times needed to find and train pilots, crew, and support technicians, the country is already developing robust and comprehensive training programs to produce aviation personnel able to operate to the high standards demanded. Once again, the country developed these programs with the end goal of attracting entrants from further afield.

In summary, the UAE's patient approach of establishing an end goal, looking at what it needs, and building the foundations for getting there is why the country's aviation industry could expand in such a short time to become a regional leader and with some of the most respected airlines in the world.

# CHAPTER 3

## EXPANDING THE AVIATION INDUSTRY

After its genesis in 1985, and supported by strong foundations and long-term planning, the UAE's aviation industry continued to expand in size and reputation. Emirates is one of the most respected in the world, with an ultra-modern fleet, and the UAE always makes sure that it anticipates any growth and makes sure it has the infrastructure to handle it well in advance.

With the initial success of Emirates Airlines, the UAE's aviation industry continued to expand with the establishment of other airlines such as Etihad Airways, Air Arabia, and FlyDubai. These airlines cater to different markets and have helped diversify the country's aviation industry.

## Expansion

By 1993, Emirates continued to be one of the fastest-growing airlines in the world, with revenue increasing by $100 million per year. The Gulf War also saw Emirates continue to grow as other airlines actively avoided the area. The airline carried 3 million passengers per year and freight traffic increased to make up 16% of its business.

In 1993, the airline offered long-haul services, in partnership with US Airways, and by 1995, with a fleet of Six Airbus A300s and eight A310s, covered 37 destinations in 30 countries. In 1996, it acquired Boeing 777-20 and six 777-20ERs, supporting long haul as far as Australia.

## Cargo

Emirates always operated a cargo service with its passenger aircraft but, in 1998, it developed freight capabilities, leasing a Boeing 747-200 freighter from Atlas Air with insurance and servicing included.

## Into the 2000s

During the 2000s, Emirates continued to expand, ordering over 50 aircraft and expanding its non-stop long-haul services, including the US, Australia, and Brazil.

In 2003, at the Paris Air Show, Emirates purchased/leased another 71 aircraft, following this, in 2005, with a purchase of 42 Boeing aircraft in a $9.7 billion deal.

In 2007, at the Dubai Air Show, the airline invested $34.9 billion in 143 new aircraft, mainly Airbus with some Boeing. Between 2009 and 2011, the company invested heavily to expand its fleet even more with over 80 Boeing 777 aircraft.

2012 saw Emirates sign a partnership with Qantas to move its hub from Singapore to Dubai and the two companies matched frequent fliers and other programs. In 2013, the company ordered 150 777 and 50 A380 aircraft, for delivery from 2020 onwards, to expand and replace aging aircraft.

In 2017, the airline purchased several aircraft from Boeing, including 40 787-10 Dreamliners as part of a $15.1 billion deal for delivery starting in 2022. Finally, the company, in 2020, moved its operations to the new Dubai World Central - Al Maktoum International Airport.

## Focusing on Excellence and Image

In the previous chapter, we looked at how developing the UAE's aviation infrastructure gave its airlines room to grow. However, that is only part of the story, and Emirates itself had to grow into that potential with a business plan and approach that focused on the most important tasks for building and expanding the company. Most of all, its executives understood the importance of excelling at those critical tasks to help the airline carve open a market and start to dominate.

To do this, Emirates focused on building a brand through aggressive marketing, developing a reputation for quality, and seeking to refine its approach wherever possible, making the small gains that add up to a positive image, public trust, and a reputation for putting passengers first. Emirates understands the importance of philanthropy and sees it as a core business principle.

## Brand Awareness

Emirates understood the importance of building brand awareness and, in 2007, purchased the naming rights for Arsenal FC's new stadium for $100 million, tapping into the lucrative Premier League market, something they would ramp up later on. The airline also built awareness through links with Real Madrid as part of an aggressive marketing campaign. Its extensive marketing campaign focuses on certain customer demographics.

The company long focused on customer satisfaction, realizing that its customers sought comfort, efficiency, and very high quality of service, especially on long haul flights. Small improvements such as Wi-Fi, better catering, and fewer delays are relatively easy to so but enhance the customer experience and build trust.

## Challenging the Status Quo

Emirates understood simple geography, noting that the UAE was in a prime location as a stopover and regional hub for flights, so the country became an integral addition to international travel routes. Emirate's strategy involved developing an international travel hub because the UAE is in a prime location between Europe, Asia, and the South Pacific, making it an optimal location at the center of a 'hub and spoke' model, especially for long haul flights.[13]

The location, within eight hours of half the world's population, means that it is perfect for flights connecting Europe, Asia, and Australia. This also helps develop the UAE's reputation as a global hub for aviation and supports the MRO companies and other services and sectors it is developing.

The growth of Emirates provides a lesson in developing strategies, especially how it continues to promote quality, luxury, and stress-free travel. The airline emphasizes customer service, ensuring that it retains customers and builds real value for the brand. If a

---

[13] Kamarudeen and Sundarakani, 2019

customer has a bad experience with an airline, they are unlikely to use it again and negative publicity can soon eat into a company's image and profitability. Safety is also important in customer perception and for any ethical business, so Emirates maintains exceptionally high safety standards.

Emirates also hires and trains skilled crews that can speak in many languages and are able to overcome cultural issues and barriers. The company also offers a website and other materials in at least 13 languages to further enhance its reputation as a truly international company.

Emirates believes in comprehensive training for all its workforce, and that paying competitive wages with a number of benefits to ensure that employee retention is high. It is better to retain employees that you have invested time and resources in rather than having a high employee turnover.

The UAE also waived visa requirements for many countries to make transit easier. Over time, the UAE has covered the entire region and widened its customer base.

## Building Success

As it grew, Emirates focused heavily on Boeing and Airbus aircraft, allowing them to build strong partnerships with the two companies. This makes maintenance and logistics for parts much easier and also means that the airline can work with the companies to develop what it needs for future growth.

Emirates Airlines adopted a number of strategies to build success, such as opting for long haul flights to reduce the costs incurred by frequent landing, taking advantage of the country's location. To help this, the airline tends to opt for wide body aircraft to maximize profit per seat, and ensuring that the average age of its aircraft is low reduces maintenance costs significantly.

Perhaps reflecting the UAE's shift towards a high-technology economy, Emirates Airlines always adopts new technologies that enhance the customer experience early. This includes booking systems, in-flight entertainment, and boarding, which help separate them from the competition.

Emirates Airlines uses competitive tendering for products and services including entertainment during flights, internet, and food among many other passenger comforts. To supplement this, Emirates has its own In-House Research Center that helps it follow continuous improvement for products and services aimed at the customer experience.

The Emirates Airlines Engineering Centre, based at Dubai International Airport, employs over 5,000 people including 1,200 engineers. The center contains hangars that allow checkup and maintenance of two aircraft at a time. Aircraft are checked frequently according to age and air miles and they have a large store of parts for maintenance due to the long lead times for parts from the USA and Europe.

The Emirates Flight Training Academy is considered one of the best pilot training academies in the world, working with Boeing, which provides software and a comprehensive training curriculum. Another way in which Emirates promotes efficiency is by having warehouses near the two major airports for spare parts and for catering to reduce logistics costs.

## Focus on the Most Important Tasks to Support Growth

As the UAE's aviation program developed and Emirates and other airlines expanded, a strategy became clear. Emirates Airlines and its associated companies focused on the most important tasks to support growth. More than that, they made sure that, for every task, there was a strong reason for doing it, a long-term strategy, and a goal to do everything well, from the basics to ensuring that the airline is seen as best in class by customers, suppliers, and other airlines.

For example, cutting costs without making unacceptable compromises was a main focus and the airline explored every option for doing this, such as streamlining logistics, focusing on fewer landings, and maximizing revenue from each seat. These small tasks add up to savings that allow the airline to profit.

The airline also understands its clientele and offers a high-quality service and comfort, for which it needs the latest technology but also a high emphasis on safety because an avoidable accident will undo all of the company's reputation. Accordingly, Emirates focuses on lowering the average age of its fleet, using thorough maintenance programs and highly trained pilots and engineers.

Focusing on few tasks but doing them well and making sure that every part of the company and infrastructure supports them is something that the UAE would carry into its burgeoning space program.

# Chapter 4

## The UAE's Ambitious Vision for Space

Over 30 years, the UAE built a successful aviation industry, developing Emirates Airline and other companies through adopting a policy of providing the infrastructure and services needed to support them. Becoming a regional aviation hub took an original vision and a strategy that focused on a vision and strategy that built strong foundation.

The aviation industry was an integral part of developing a diversified economy built upon technology and a well-educated, highly trained workforce. Accordingly, it is no surprise that, given the attachment of the UAE's leaders to space, the country started using the expertise gained building its aerospace industry to take the next step. Now, the UAE has embraced the space race and has made significant strides in the past decade. In the same way, the country has set up funding and specialist organizations developed to achieve the visions.

The country intends to become a world leader in the space industry and is increasing its influence through satellite technology, space exploration, and a number of other sectors related to the industry. The UAE's vision for space lays out in detail how it will create expertise and a whole industry geared towards economic diversification and a skill-based economy. Now, the country has the UAE Space Agency, with a goal to advance the country's space exploration and development capabilities.

The UAE's development of its space sector uses a very similar playbook to the aviation industry and can build upon the work already achieved in building infrastructure and training centers, finding partners and, most of all, focusing on the building blocks it needs to bring the vision to reality.

Already, the UAE wishes to send a mission to Mars in the next century and every action it takes shifts progress inexorably towards that goal, from building satellites and sending probes to sending Emirati astronauts into space and building a spaceport. To achieve these goals, the country's leaders created policies and guidance that shape the approach and help all of the elements needed move in the same direction and end goal.

## Policies and Guidance

Just with the aviation program, the UAE's space program did not emerge from nowhere without any direction. Instead, it follows a process based upon setting ambitious goals and developing thorough but flexible plans for getting there. These lay out the vision and also show how the space program fits into the plans for the future of the country's economy and position as a leading technological hub.

Using a very similar blueprint to the aviation and aerospace program, the UAE's leaders understood the importance of steady growth under an organization that oversees all of the organizations and people involved to guide them towards the goals. Accordingly, in 2006, the country set up a space center followed by the UAE Space Agency in 2014.

In 2006, Sheikh Mohammed Bin Rashid, Prime Minister of the UAE and ruler of Dubai founded the MBRSC, integrating it with the Emirates Institution for Advanced Science & Technology (EIAST). [14] The organization is owned by the government and promotes space science in the region

In 2014, building upon a series of announcements that the UAE had already released about its space program, the UAE's president, Highness Sheikh Khalifa bin Zayed Al Nahyan, issued a decree. This set up the UAE Space Agency that reported directly to the cabinet but had financial, administrative, and a large degree of political independence.

The mandate of this new agency was to gather together all of the existing programs and organizations contributing to the UAE's developing space sector. Overall, the Space Agency's mandate was to:

*"Develop, organize, support, guide and coordinate the UAE's growing Space sector that contributes to a diversified UAE national economy and which supports sustainable development."*

From the start, the UAE's Space Agency had a number of responsibilities towards the wider drive into space:

- Increase national awareness of the importance of the space program
- Develop a skilled and qualified workforce.
- Develop space policies and regulations as well as enforce them.

---

[14] Space science and technology, *UAE Government,* https://u.ae/en/about-the-uae/science-and-technology/key-sectors-in-science-and-technology/space-science-and-technology

- Help the UAE become an internationally recognized contributor to aerospace
- Foster international partnerships to facilitate knowledge transfer

In addition to this, the Space Agency embraced the UAE's existing space programs, supporting them and maximizing the chances of success. The UAE Space Agency directs the national space program as part of the UAE's economic diversification strategy, helping to position the UAE as a leading global aerospace hub.[15]

Now, with the responsibility of directing the country's space program and creating policies, the agency began its work, developing goals that not only laid out a direction of travel for the burgeoning space industry, but also ensuring that they fitted into the UAE's wider goals for economic diversification and cultural shift to a technological, knowledge-based economy.

Very quickly, the UAE's Space Agency applied for membership of the International Space Exploration Coordination Group, becoming the first Arab country accepted.

The new agencies responsibilities and growing number of partnerships and programs clearly needed direction and focus. Accordingly, to provide a framework, the Space Agency released its National Space Policy document in 2016, to coordinate the space program and also set down its aims and goals.

---

[15] Saikali, 2022

## UAE Space Policy

The UAE's National Space Policy, a comprehensive policy document, set out the UAE's ambitions and approach to the new space industry, and showed how it would manage and coordinate efforts as well as find synergies with other national programs.[16] The comprehensive policy followed a period of discussion and consultation with other governmental entities, and international organizations as well as absorbing international best practices int the core of the document.

The policy sprang from the UAE's wider Vision 2021 program that discussed a Higher Policy for Science, Technology and Innovation, and the National Innovation Strategy.

The National Space Policy document embraced some key principles that shaped the space program, establishing who and what it was for, and how it would benefit the UAE. Some of the core principles included:

- Enrich the life of the UAE's citizens
- Increase knowledge of the universe
- Improve education and increase scientific study and research
- Increase the number of skilled jobs for nationals
- Create a sense of national pride

---

[16] UAE National Space Policy, *UAE Government,* September 2016, https://space.gov.ae/Documents/PublicationPDFFiles/UAE_National_Space_Policy_English.pdf

The policy also aligned with a number of national policies intended to increase the stability and security of the UAE by supporting growth and economic diversification. A space policy built upon innovation and a sustainable space sector will support these and help the UAE develop the knowledge base it needs. Importantly, the policy ensured that the UAE's space program followed all relevant international space treaties.

As with many national space programs, 'soft influence' is important, and the policy document understands the importance of developing international partnerships. Working with neighbours and allies for the benefit of all will help to improve the global standing of the country and the wider region.

## UAE Space Program

In 2017, the UAE announced its ambitious space program laying out its vision for the future.[17] The Space Program drew heavily upon the UAE's ambitions and how it would carve out a path. Far from being a project in vanity, the UAE's space program showed how it would support other sectors and goals, creating value beyond the program.

The space program would help the UAE economically and politically, as well as contributing to national security and other initiatives.

---

[17] Mohammed bin Rashid, Abu Dhabi Crown Prince launch National Space Program, *WAM,* https://wam.ae/en/details/1395302608363

For example, the program embraced using satellite technology for agriculture and climate modelling, as well as helping with disaster recovery and supporting broadcasting and communications.

As is common with Emirati initiatives, the program sought to attract international investment and resources through creating the right regulatory environment and allowing private business and entrepreneurs to make meaningful contributions. The plan also showed how the country would develop space engineers, scientists, astronomers, and other professionals able to work in the space industry and increase the UAE's reputation as a global space hub. This included the National Space Program, in 2017, with the intent of training young Emiratis. [18]

The program also solidified the UAE's commitment to a number of space missions, including its Hope Mission to Mars and astronaut program. Overall, the UAE wants to adopt a leading regional and international role in space exploration and within the international space community. Soon afterwards, the UAE built upon its space program with a new national space strategy.

## National Space Strategy 2030

The National Space Strategy 2030 further supports the UAE's ambition to develop a space program and new technologies. [19] It also integrates with the National Space Policy and a number of other

---

[18] Saikali, Sussan, The UAE Looks to the Stars, *The Arab Gulf States Institution in Washington,* August 16, 2022, https://agsiw.org/the-uae-looks-to-the-stars/

[19] UAE Cabinet approves National Space Strategy 2030, *Government of Dubai,* March 11, 2019, https://www.mediaoffice.ae/en/news/2019/3/UAE-Cabinet-approves-National-Space-Strategy-2030

initiatives intended to upskill and diversify the UAE's economy, such as UAE Vision 2021 and Centennial Plan 2071.[20]

The main goal of the 2030 strategy is to take the goals and ambitions from the National Space Policy and create a number of Areas of Focus. The plan lays out how the government would support the space industry through a number of initiatives and bring together public, private, and academic input to grow the sector. The strategy showed how and where the UAE could expand the sector, seek commercial opportunities, and work with international partners.[21]

With six overall objectives, 21 different programs, and 79 initiatives, the 2030 strategy will benefit over 85 UAE entities. At the same time, the UAE made it easier for entrepreneurs and other people who can contribute to its plans gain longer term visas.[22] Naturally, this ambitious program required funding, so the government laid out a number of financial support packages for the space program.

## National Space Fund

The UAE set up an AED 3 billion (US $817 million) national space fund to support international and Emirati companies cooperating for space sector engineering and science research. It will enhance Emirati capabilities and contribute to diversification of the economy.

---

[20] National Space Strategy (Summary) 2030, *UAE Space Agency,*
https://space.gov.ae/Documents/PublicationPDFFiles/2030-National-Strategy-Summary-EN.pdf
[21] https://space.gov.ae/Documents/PublicationPDFFiles/2030-National-Strategy-Summary-EN.pdf
[22] https://gulfnews.com/uae/science/uae-cabinet-approves-national-space-strategy-2030-1.62589230

In particular, the fund is intended to help develop the necessary infrastructure alongside developing startups and attracting global expertise.[23]

The fund will prioritize educational programs and seek to support innovation and training, as well as continuing the policy of developing partnerships with international technology companies and attracting investment from abroad.

## Space Economic Zones Program

In a similar vein to the Al Maktoum International Airport, which intends to create an aviation hub with all relevant businesses and entities close together, the UAE wants to set up Space Economic Zones, and initiated a program The SEZ program will help SMEs contribute to the national space program through knowledge sharing, partnerships, and financial support.[24]

The first of these was at Masdar City, announced in 2022, where the UAESA created a package to help startups and SMEs incubate and grow as part of an interconnected business ecosystem. Announced at the start of 2022, this space industry hub offers excellent supporting infrastructure and an interconnected business environment designed to attract startups.

Alongside the infrastructure, the SEZ supports a simple, fast track system for licensing and visas for foreign workers for companies working in all aspects of the space industry, from engineering and

---

[23] Space science and technology, *UAE*, https://u.ae/en/about-the-uae/science-and-technology/key-sectors-in-science-and-technology/space-science-and-technology
[24] Space Economic Zones Program, *UAE Space Agency*, *https://space.gov.ae/Page/20121/20268/Space-Economic-Zones-Program*

software to logistics. Importantly, understanding the need to support and nurture these businesses, Masdar encourages networking, mentoring, and links with world leading research centers.[25] A space law, passed in 2019, already facilitates visas and business permits for companies working within the space industry. [26]

Alongside Masdar city, other SEZs include Mars Science City, Nibras Al Ain Aerospace Park, and Dubai South. [27]Other similar SEZs in Dubai, Abu Dhabi, and Sharjah will further help startups and SMEs contribute to the space program, bringing the private sector into the fold. The process is very similar to the public-private links developed by NASA in the US, which try to encourage companies to develop new technologies with support.[28]

## Financial Support

So far, the UAE has invested over $400 million in its space industry and intends to double that over the next decade. [29] Companies can apply for funding from a Space Analytics and Solutions initiative developed by the UAESA to cultivate space

---

[25] https://news.masdar.ae/en/News/2022/09/21/06/34/Masdar-City-and-the-UAE-Space-Agency-Announce-new-Package

[26] https://www.thenationalnews.com/uae/uae-in-space/2022/04/04/how-the-uae-plans-to-become-a-big-space-power-in-the-region/

[27]

https://space.gov.ae/Documents/PublicationPDFFiles/Space_Invest_Plan_EN_Summary_042020.pdf

[28] https://www.thenationalnews.com/uae/uae-in-space/2022/04/04/how-the-uae-plans-to-become-a-big-space-power-in-the-region/

[29] https://www.thenationalnews.com/uae/uae-in-space/2022/04/04/how-the-uae-plans-to-become-a-big-space-power-in-the-region/

programs that focus on climate change, agriculture and food security, and other industries.

These funds will taper off as businesses become self-funding over time. The idea is that the fund will reduce risk and offer support as NASA did with SpaceX, helping companies start but encouraging them to innovate and develop rather than risk stagnation if they become too dependent on funding.[30]

## Space Investment Promotion Plan

The UAE's Space Investment Promotion Plan is intended to support the national space policy and help the country achieve all the goals laid out in the UAE Vision 2021 and other plans. Again, it supports economic diversification, a knowledge-based economy, and encouraging R&D innovation, especially in the private sector.[31]

The plan will drive the growth of the UAE space industry and support the industrial ecosystem, creating new businesses and jobs as well as attracting international businesses and investment. The fund also intends to support increased education in STEM subjects and developing a skilled workforce.

The fund will also look to attract partnerships with international partnerships covering the public, private, and academic sectors to encourage R&D and gradually increase the reputation of the UAE as a destination for the space industry. This includes creating a

---

[30] https://www.thenationalnews.com/uae/uae-in-space/2022/04/04/how-the-uae-plans-to-become-a-big-space-power-in-the-region/

[31]

https://space.gov.ae/Documents/PublicationPDFFiles/Space_Invest_Plan_EN_Summary_042020.pdf transparent and fair regulatory environment for foreign and local companies, and further supporting the SEZs, creating logistics hubs and potentially a space port.

## Space Ventures

The Space Ventures program, announced by the MBRSC in 2021, will link the space sector around the world and create an environment for innovative startups.[32] The Space Ventures initiative is funded ICT Fund of the Telecommunications and Digital Government Regulatory Authority.[33] The ICT Fund, headed up by Omar Almahmoud as the current CEO, is a federal development fund launched by the UAE's Telecommunications Regulatory Authority with purpose of catalyzing the ICT sector in the UAE through investments in education, R&D, incubation and national technology initiatives, such as Space. The fund has a determined mission to provide strategic targeted funding to empower and develop innovation and build a knowledge based economy for the UAE.

Businesses will be able to work with MBRSC to develop longer term projects and access support and technology from agencies and academics around the world. These partnerships will help promising startups and the wider economy, creating a competitive space market in the UAE and the Gulf region as a whole.

---

[32] Saikali, 2022

[33] Dubai's MBRSC creates UAE space sector launchpad for start-ups, *Arabian Business,* October 21, 2021, https://www.arabianbusiness.com/startup/469872-dubais-mbrsc-creates-launchpad-for-start-ups-in-the-uae-space-industry

Some of the sectors covered in the program include IT, communications, satellite technology, robotics, and a number of other fields that the space program needs. Companies accessing the program must be based in the UAE. [34]

## Hub 71

Hub 71, an Abu Dhabi initiative, intends to promote the high technology sector. This includes space tech startups, giving them help and support. It helps companies in a number of sectors access global marketplaces, find investors, and build partnerships. By 2022, Hub71, partly owned by Mubadala and working with Masdar, had helped over 200 startups.[35,36]

## UAE Space Law

Developing a space industry requires a regulatory and legal environment that oversees all aspects, so the UAE developed a framework covering all aspects of the National Space Policy. Some of the areas covered include finance and environmental laws. With this, companies and investors are much more confident and willing to contribute to the space program.

## Training and Infrastructure

---

[34] Dubai's MBRSC creates UAE space sector launchpad for start-ups, *Arabian Business,* October 21, 2021, https://www.arabianbusiness.com/startup/469872-dubais-mbrsc-creates-launchpad-for-start-ups-in-the-uae-space-industry

[35] Saikali, 2022

[36] Cresniov, Alex, As UAE's space sector grows in stature, SpaceTech fund and accelerator are natural next steps, *Arabian Business,* March 24, 2022, https://www.arabianbusiness.com/opinion/as-uaes-space-sector-grows-in-stature-spacetech-fund-and-accelerator-are-natural-next-steps

As with the aviation industry, setting up infrastructure and developing a well-trained workforce with all of the skills and knowledge needed to help the space industry thrive is crucial. The UAE is actively encouraging education in fields related to aerospace, and has set up a number of training initiatives to help it develop the skills it needs. Policies to encourage knowledge sharing between public bodies, the private sector, and academia are particularly important.

One such program is the Arab Space Discovery Program which, as part of the National Space Program, will transfer space science knowledge between Arab institutions and universities.[37] The Arab Space Pioneers Program, set up in 2020, will help Arab engineers, scientists, inventors, and researchers gain the skills they need to enter the space program.[38]

In 2015, a memorandum between Yahsat, Masdar Institute of Science and Technology and Orbital ATK created a Degree Program in Advanced Space Science. With input from UAESA, the training will take place at Masdar. The first graduates emerged in 2018.[39] They have a range of skills suited to working in all areas of the aerospace industry[40]

---

[37] National Space Programme, *UAE Government,* https://u.ae/en/about-the-uae/strategies-initiatives-and-awards/strategies-plans-and-visions/industry-science-and-technology/national-space-programme

[38] In the run up to the first Arab probe lift-off to Mars, VP launches 'Arab Space Pioneers' programme, *WAM,* July 4, 2020, https://wam.ae/en/details/1395302853057

[39] Masdar Institute's Pioneering Space Graduates Ready to Launch, *Khalifa University,* September 21, 2018, https://www.ku.ac.ae/masdar-institute-s-pioneering-space-graduates-ready-to-launch

[40] Master's Concentration in Space Systems and Technology, *Masdar Institute of Science and Technology,* http://ednet.ae/masdar-institute-of-science-and-

Finally, the Space Workshops, provided an extensive two-week training course for young Emiratis interested in STEM and seeking a career in aerospace and the space industry. [41]

## Collaborate and Look for Win-Win Collaboration

This idea of collaboration, between the private and public sectors, and bringing in academia and R&D, is one of the cornerstones of the UAE's space industry and its development. Collaboration with international companies is also very important, building upon the experience with the aviation industry.

International investment brings technology and knowledge alongside finance, and it also increases the reputation of the UAE and its growing space industry. Space is one of the most internationalized fields and building collaboration across boundaries is crucial if the UAE is to thrive. A number of policies within the UAE support this outward-looking philosophy.

The UAE also points out that its space program is about Arab countries, and that the UAE's success in space are successes for the entire region. By doing this, the UAE can present itself as a leader in the region and help to promote greater cooperation. [42]

---

technology/engineering/civil-engineering/masters-concentration-in-space-systems-and-technology

[41] Emirati Graduates complete Phase I of Space Workshops, *Times Aerospace,* February 8, 2023, https://www.timesaerospace.aero/news/space/emirati-graduates-complete-phase-i-of-space-workshops

[42] Mohammed Soliman, The geopolitics of space: Why did the UAE send a probe to Mars?, *Middle East Institute,* March 25, 2021, https://www.mei.edu/publications/geopolitics-space-why-did-uae-send-probe-mars

# Chapter 5

## Mohammed Bin Rashid Space Centre and the UAE Space Agency Programs

The UAE has patiently developed the infrastructure and organizations needed to develop a space program and already took its first steps. Starting with a few Earth orbit satellites, the country has now sent several missions into space, looking towards the moon, Mars, and even the asteroid belt. In just a few decades, the country has started realizing the visions of its founders.

As laid out in its space policies, the UAE wishes to establish itself as a regional hub for civil and commercial space activities. The UAE Space Agency (UAESA) and Mohammed Bin Rashid Space Centre (MBRSC) are playing a leading role, overseeing a number of programs that have put the policies into practice and helped the country develop skilled technicians, engineers, professionals, and astronauts for the space programs.

Importantly, these high-profile programs created interest among the public, encouraging young Emiratis to see the space industry as a career. The UAESA created links with a number of universities and institutions to create a pool of expertise and give practical experience.

**Universities and Institutions**

Although UAESA works with a number of academic institutions, two universities stand out.

Khalifa University is at the forefront of the UAE's space program, and opened the Spacecraft Platform for Astronautic and Celestial Emulation (SPACE) laboratory in 2015.

The UAE University in Al-Ai hosts the National Space Science and Technology Center, which performs research into CubeSats and likely conditions on Mars.

Looking further afield, to the Global Alliance of Earth Observation Satellites Operators (PanGeo), the Emirates Institution for Advanced Science and Technology (EISAT) was one of the first signatories to the program. PanGeo is a collaboration between a number of space agencies to share data and images from their satellites. [43]

## Satellite Programs

Although the UAE's leaders have very strong ambitions for the space program that include space expeditions and sending Emiratis into space, satellite programs have been very important. The UAE understands the importance of remote sensing through satellites for monitoring land use, climate monitoring, and many other applications. [44]

In addition, these satellite programs help the country develop the skills and test the technology it will need for more complicated

---

[43] EIAST joins global satellite alliance PanGeo, *Times Aerospace,* February 10, 2014, https://www.timesaerospace.aero/news/space/eiast-joins-global-satellite-alliance-pangeo
[44] Cresniov, Alex, As UAE's space sector grows in stature, SpaceTech fund and accelerator are natural next steps, *Arabian Business,* March 24, 2022, https://www.arabianbusiness.com/opinion/as-uaes-space-sector-grows-in-stature-spacetech-fund-and-accelerator-are-natural-next-steps

missions. Mubadala has been particularly prominent in driving progress and oversees a number of programs.

## Advanced Aerial Systems Programme

EISAT established the Advanced Aerial Systems program to promote design, manufacture, and operation of aerial systems. The High Altitude Pseudo Satellite (HAPS) system was the first AAS project. It is a vehicle that flies above the stratosphere using only solar power, remaining airborne for weeks. In can perform imaging, thermal imaging, and even provide temporary communications.[45]

Another AAS project, EIAST's Super Resolution Tool, enhances satellite imagery and resolution to support zooming in. Created by an Emirati engineer, SRT improves the detail of images taken by satellites, helping to improve the contrast and help with land use monitoring.[46]

## Yahsat Communication Satellites

Yahsat, a subsidiary of Mubadala Investment Company, operates a number of communications satellites, including the Al Yah satellites launched by Arianespace and Thuraya satellites built by Boeing.[47,48] Its communication satellites cover two-thirds of the world's

---

[45] EIAST launches its Advanced Aerial Systems Program, *WAM*, September 24, 2014

[46] Howard, Courtney, EIAST launches Super Resolution Tool to enhance resolution, clarity of satellite images, *Military Aerospace*, May 14, 2012, https://www.militaryaerospace.com/commercial-aerospace/article/14227695/eiast-launches-super-resolution-tool-to-enhance-resolution-clarity-of-satellite-images

[47] UAE Country Commercial Guide: Space, *US Trade Administration*, 26 July, 2022, https://www.trade.gov/country-commercial-guides/united-arab-emirates-space

[48] Connecting Communities Across the Globe, *Yahsat*, https://www.yahsat.com/en/about-yahsat/our-fleet

population and helps the company offer communications solutions for companies and governments.

Yahsat provides a perfect example of how the UAE's space industry can support other sectors such as communications, helping the sector grow and encourage more companies to invest. Yahsat launched a number of satellites over the past few years, each showing how much the Emirati space program is progressing.

## Earth Monitoring Satellites

DubaiSat-1 and DubaiSat-2, developed with South Korean company, Satrec Initiative, a satellite manufacturer, was built by the Emirates Institution for Advanced Science and Technology (EIAST), part of the MBRSC.[49] Launched in 2009 and 2013, the satellites produce mid-resolution imagery that supported urban planning, including Al Maktoum Airport. The DubaiSats also monitor weather patterns and environmental change, as well as helping with international disaster relief efforts.[50,51]

Launched in Japan in 2018, KhalifaSat was the first satellite designed, built, and tested in the UAE entirely by Emirati scientists and engineers. Using a digital camera, it monitors environmental changes and helps with urban management and planning. [52]

---

[49] https://www.thenationalnews.com/uae/science/2021/12/21/mbz-sat-uae-space-centre-to-start-building-regions-most-advanced-imaging-satellite/

[50] https://www.mbrsc.ae/portfolio/dubaisat-1/

[51] https://www.mbrsc.ae/portfolio/dubaisat-2/

[52] 10 Things You Should Know About the UAE Space Program, *Smithsonian Magazine,* 2019, https://www.smithsonianmag.com/sponsored/10-Things-to-Know-UAE-Space-Program-Future-Space-Exploration-180971672/

KhalifaSat is part of MBRSC's drive to contribute to a high-technology economy by developing skills and inspiring innovation.[53]

Supported by the National Space Fund, the Constellation of Advanced Imaging Satellites (Sirb) will develop and launch a series of imaging satellites. They will create radar images of land use and monitor land use, using Synthetic Aperture Radar) technology to peer through clouds and fog. It is a collaboration between public and private sectors, including international collaborations.[54,55,56]

Finally, MBZ-SAT, to be launched in 2023, will be the Next Generation Earth Observation satellite. [57] The satellite is a collaboration between five companies, including Strata, and 90% of the mechanical systems and 50% of the electronics will be built in the UAE. The new satellite will be three times more efficient than KhalifaSat and produce ten times the number of images. It will also send information via the downlink three times faster.

Notably, the project includes over 100 engineers and used international experts.[58] For MBZ-Sat, the UAE is trying to convince

---

[53] UAE Country Commercial Guide: Space, *US Trade Administration*, 26 July, 2022, https://www.trade.gov/country-commercial-guides/united-arab-emirates-space

[54] Space science and technology, *UAE*, https://u.ae/en/about-the-uae/science-and-technology/key-sectors-in-science-and-technology/space-science-and-technology

[55] UAE to develop and launch advanced radar satellite constellation under new AED3 billion space sector fund, *WAM*, July 17, 2022, https://wam.ae/en/details/1395303066705

[56] https://www.zawya.com/en/press-release/government-news/united-arab-emirates-to-develop-and-launch-advanced-radar-satellite-constellation-under-new-aed3bln-space-sector-fund-yw47zwcv

[57] UAE Country Commercial Guide: Space, *US Trade Administration*, 26 July, 2022, https://www.trade.gov/country-commercial-guides/united-arab-emirates-space

[58] https://www.thenationalnews.com/uae/science/2021/12/21/mbz-sat-uae-space-centre-to-start-building-regions-most-advanced-imaging-satellite/

existing companies of the benefits of moving into the space sector and the potential for growth.

## Educational Satellite Programs

The UAE understands the importance of the satellite program as a way to engage young Emiratis and help them develop the skills they need to work in the aerospace industry. Accordingly, two satellites worked closely with academic institutions to support students in every stage of satellite development, from concept and design to manufacture and launch.

Launched on February 15, 2017, NAYIF-1 is the UAE's first nanosatellite and resulted from a collaboration between MBRSC and academic institutions such as the American University of Sharjah (AUS) The project provides a prime example of knowledge sharing and collaboration. This small satellite, launched on an Indian rocket and helped Emirati engineering students develop the skills and practical experience they need to design, develop, and manufacture small satellites.[59]

MeznSat also helped to engage young Emiratis to participate, a continuous theme of the UAE's space program. To find young engineers and designers, the UAE established the Mini Satellite Challenge, working with Boeing. The intent of the challenge was to encourage young graduates and undergraduates at Khalifa University

---

[59] https://www.mbrsc.ae/portfolio/nayif

to design satellites. The resulting MeznSat will monitor climate change in the country.[60,61,62]

## Space Exploration

The UAE built up its space industry and capability gradually, supporting its ambitions and overall vision, but always patiently building solid foundations. Ambition is essential but can lead nowhere if it does not have support and the resources to succeed.

With the work undertaken to develop an infrastructure, build upon the experience gained with aviation, and plans to develop the right environment and support, the UAE looked to the next stage. Space exploration and sending missions to the moon and planets charted by their ancestors became a national goal.

In 2018, at the International Astronautical Conference and the Artemis Accords, UAESC signed NASA's Artemis Accords at the 71st International Astronautical Conference, one of the first space agencies to do so. The Artemis Accords promote a shared vision for space and principles that promise space exploration based upon peace and sharing.[63] The UAE later hosted the IAC in October 2021.

As with all of its space projects, the UAE built up partnerships, attracted international expertise, and used the program as a learning

---

[60] 10 Things You Should Know About the UAE Space Program, 2019

[61] Nazir, Sarwhat, Mini satellite developed by UAE students to launch this month, *The National,* September 14, 2020, https://www.thenationalnews.com/uae/science/mini-satellite-developed-by-uae-students-to-launch-this-month-1.1077538

[62] https://www.thenationalnews.com/uae/uae-in-space/2022/04/04/how-the-uae-plans-to-become-a-big-space-power-in-the-region/

[63] https://www.nasa.gov/specials/artemis-accords/img/Artemis-Accords-signed-13Oct2020.pdf

experience for Emirati engineers, scientists, and technicians. The UAEs first steps beyond Earth orbit were the lunar missions, which showed the country's ambition and willingness to succeed.

## Lunar Missions

The UAE set its sights on Earth's closest neighbor, seeing missions to the moon as the first stage of space exploration and helping the country become a recognized space-faring nation.

The Emirates Lunar Mission, overseen by the MBRSC, was the first UAE mission to the moon and included the Rashid lander, intended to study the surface of the moon. Sadly, the Japanese Nakuto-R lander failed just before touchdown on April 25, 2023.[64]

The rover, which would have made the UAE only the fourth country to land on the moon, was intended to study soil, geology, and dust on the moon.[65] While the failure was a setback, the UAE already has other missions under development and its space exploration program continues.

In 2021, the UAE signed an agreement to work with Israeli company SpaceIL on the Beresheet 2 Moon Mission, cooperating on design and research for a new satellite to study the moon.[66] The mission intends to promote cooperation between the countries and

---

[64] UAE Space Exploration, *UAE USA United,* https://www.uaeusaunited.com/stories/uae-space-exploration

[65] https://gulfnews.com/uae/science/emirates-lunar-mission-all-eyes-on-the-moon-as-uaes-rashid-rover-attempts-lunar-landing-on-april-25-1.1682351235528

[66] Saikali, 2022

will include a landing and a satellite, and will engage Israeli and Emirati students.[67]

## Interplanetary Missions

Looking beyond the moon and seeking to fulfil the original visions of the country's space program, the UAESA looked further into the solar system, at Mars, Venus, and the chaotic asteroid belt. Soon, a number of missions emerged, each designed to promote domestic industry and help to develop expertise.

In 2006, the UAE began seeking the knowledge it needed to prepare for missions to Mars. [68] Reaching the Red Planet is undoubtedly one of the main ambitions of the UAE's space program and inspired the imagination of its leaders. Alongside its growing space industry and development of expertise, missions to Mars emerged in the national consciousness in 2014, with the announcement of the Hope Mission.

### *AMAL/HOPE PROBE*

Showing the increasing ability of its private space sector, the UAE announced its Hope Mission in 2014, with the intention of reaching the planet in 2021, the Golden Jubilee of the country's founding. [69]In 2021, the Hope Probe arrived at Mars to measure how

---

[67] https://www.jpost.com/middle-east/article-705511

[68] 10 Things You Should Know About the UAE Space Program, 2019

[69] https://www.thenationalnews.com/uae/uae-in-space/2022/04/04/how-the-uae-plans-to-become-a-big-space-power-in-the-region/

the climate changes over time. It is surveying the atmosphere to determine if Mars could ever have supported life.[70,71]

The program was managed by the UAE with input from an international team of scientists and engineers, while The MBRSC and UAESA collaborated on the program.[72,73,74] To maximize the chance of success, the UAE worked with a number of institutions including University of Colorado Boulder, University of California, Berkeley and Arizona State University.[75]

Notably, the UAE became only the second country after India to reach Mars orbit on its first attempt. The mission showed that the UAE has the ability to develop and manage complex space missions, with over 200 Emirati engineers involved.[76]

The Hope spacecraft proved to be extremely successful, sending down data from the Martian atmosphere and making new discoveries contributing to our understanding of the planet. It found traces of the planet's ancient magnetic field and variations in gases in the atmosphere. For the UAE, this showed that the country's space

---

[70] 10 Things You Should Know About the UAE Space Program, 2019

[71] Sarwat, Nasir, UAE Mars mission: history made as Hope probe successfully enters orbit, *The National,* February 9, 2021, https://www.thenationalnews.com/uae/science/uae-mars-mission-history-made-as-hope-probe-successfully-enters-orbit-1.1163202

[72] Hope, the United Arab Emirates' Mars mission, *The Planetary Society,* 2022, https://www.planetary.org/space-missions/uae-hope

[73] Al Awadhi, Mohsen, The EMM's Hope: Novel discoveries and a changing orbit set to contribute more unprecedented data to the space community, *Space.com,* April 2023, https://www.space.com/uae-hope-mars-orbiter-discoveries-op-ed

[74] UAE Country Commercial Guide: Space, *US Trade Administration,* 26 July, 2022, https://www.trade.gov/country-commercial-guides/united-arab-emirates-space

[75] UAE Space Exploration, *UAE USA United,* https://www.uaeusaunited.com/stories/uae-space-exploration

[76] https://www.mei.edu/publications/geopolitics-space-why-did-uae-send-probe-mars

program was serious and would contribute to the exploration of space. [77]

Showing how the UAE's series of initiatives to develop expertise within the private sector is having an effect, one of the local companies manufacturing components had no previous experience but used the government contract to diversify and develop new skills.

Of course, another benefit of the Hope Program is that it captured the imagination of the public and stimulated interest in space, which will hopefully encourage young Emiratis to pursue a career in the sector.

## *VENUS AND THE ASTEROID BELT*

In October 2021, the UAE Space Agency announced a plan for an Emirati interplanetary mission that would explore Venus and the asteroid belt. It should launch in 2028 and is part of the Projects of the 50 Initiative intended to commemorate the country's 50th anniversary. For this project, the UAE is partnering with the Laboratory for Atmospheric and Space Physics (LASP) at the University of Colorado, Boulder.[78,79]

The spacecraft that will explore a number of asteroids with a flyby of Venus. Importantly, it will be almost entirely built by private sector companies and will help the country strengthen its technological base. As was the case with the Mars mission, the UAE

---

[77] Kluger, Jeffrey, Sarah Al Amiri: The Woman Who Took the U.A.E. to Mars, *TIME,* February 24, 2022, https://time.com/6150593/sarah-al-amiri-mars/

[78] UAE Space Exploration, *UAE USA United,* https://www.uaeusaunited.com/stories/uae-space-exploration

[79] UAE Space Agency announces new Emirati interplanetary mission, *WAM,* October 5, 2021, https://wam.ae/en/details/1395302977188

wants to encourage established private companies to move into the space sector.[80] The probe, to be launched in 2028, will attempt to land on the final asteroid.[81]

As with many Emirati space programs, the program is intended to build expertise in engineering and scientific research in the UAE and create opportunities for the country's private sector.[82]

*MARS 2117*

The Hope Mission was the first stage of the UAE's exploration of Mars, and the country's leaders and space agency have much more ambitious programs in mind. With the intent of setting up a permanent habitable base on Mars by 2117, the UAE is building Mars Science City with laboratories and testing facilities to work towards that long time goal.[83,84]

The first stage of the program is about developing the skills and knowledge through partnerships with international research institutions and looking for better ways to travel to Mars, initially building the base with robots. To promote the program, the UAE, for the World Government Summit, produced a pamphlet imaging

---

[80] https://www.thenationalnews.com/uae/uae-in-space/2022/04/04/how-the-uae-plans-to-become-a-big-space-power-in-the-region/

[81] https://www.thenationalnews.com/uae/2022/03/29/uaes-mission-to-asteroid-belt-and-venus-moves-another-step-closer/

[82] Emirati Interplanetary Mission 2028, UAE, https://u.ae/en/about-the-uae/uae-in-the-future/initiatives-of-the-next-50/projects-of-the-50/emirati-interplanetary-mission-2028

[83] 10 Things You Should Know About the UAE Space Program, *Smithsonian Magazine,* 2019, https://www.smithsonianmag.com/sponsored/10-Things-to-Know-UAE-Space-Program-Future-Space-Exploration-180971672/

[84] VP, Abu Dhabi Crown Prince launch AED 500 mn Mars Science City at UAE Government Annual Meetings, *WAM,* September 26, 2017, https://wam.ae/en/details/1395302634766

life on Mars for the first colonists, tapping into imagination and selling the vision. This vision is accompanied by a comprehensive VR tour.[85]

## Space Tourism

Another way in which the UAE intends to build its space industry is through encouraging space tourism. Perhaps more than any other sector, this builds directly on the infrastructure and knowledge gained through the expansion of the aviation industry. Space tourism is a growing industry worldwide and the UAE intends to capture part of that market.

The UAE is a prime location for space tourism due to its climate, which allows flights all year round, and is relatively easy for tourists to reach from Europa and Asia using the existing airport infrastructure. When added to the thriving tourist industry, hotels, and growing space industry, the country has much to offer.

Space tourism shows the value of building gradually towards a goal because the country already has most of the elements in place to attract companies wishing to operate space flights. Its satellite program and other research creates synergies with research flights and could further enhance the UAE's growing reputation as a country with an ambitious and well-resourced space program. [86]

---

[85] Al Gergawi, Saeed, Mars 2117, *World Government Summit,*
https://mars2117.worldgovernmentsummit.org/
[86] Hazlett, A. and Sheldon, J., Why the UAE can become a major space tourism hub, *Khaleej Times,* November 1, 2022, https://www.khaleejtimes.com/opinion/why-the-uae-can-become-a-major-space-tourism-hub

In March 2019, the UAE Space Agency signed an agreement with Abu Dhabi Airports over the potential use of Al Ain International Airport as a space port, with Virgin Galactic and other companies looking at opportunities to develop space tourism in the region. [87]

Some companies are already looking at the UAE, including Virgin Galactic and Blue Origin. In 2009, the government backed investment agency, Aabar Investments, bought a stake in Virgin Galactic. In 2014, Virgin discussed a potential spaceport in Abu Dhabi, and in 2020, Mubadala bought a 7% stake in the company. [88]

In 2021, the Ministry of Economy announced potentially developing a spaceport to bring Jeff Bezo's Blue Origins company to the country with a base for space tourism. [89]

## Synergize and Integrate Resources

The UAE's space program, just like the aviation and aerospace programs before it, provides a lesson in synergizing and integrating resources. All the way through the program, the government sought to create links between the public and private sectors.

In its National Space Policy, setting up the UAE Space Agency ensured that every element of the program worked towards common goals. Importantly, the program built upon the existing aviation

---

[87] 10 Things You Should Know About the UAE Space Program, 2019
[88] UAE Country Commercial Guide: Space, *US Trade Administration*, 26 July, 2022, https://www.trade.gov/country-commercial-guides/united-arab-emirates-space
[89] UAE Country Commercial Guide: Space, 2022

infrastructure, understanding that much of the infrastructure, skills, and technologies transfer between the two to create synergies.

Using economic zones and forming clusters encourages startups and ensures that they mutually support each other and have goals to work towards. Existing companies working in other sectors found opportunities for growth by accepting contracts for components of the space program and will also benefit from young Emirati graduates with relevant skills as the academic sector sees a growth in STEM programs.

Importantly, the UAE does not isolate its space program and understands that it is part of a wider goal to diversify its economy and attract investment and knowledge. For example, selling the UAE as a destination for space tourism relies upon the recent growth in the wider tourist industry, especially the luxury end, and the high reputation of the UAE's airlines for quality. Using bodies like Mubadala and investment funds also supports this integration of resources in line with wider goals.

The UAE's space program, as with many of its development programs, actively seeks links with international organizations and companies. Working with other countries and space agencies supports a pooling of resources and knowledge, as well as promoting the UAE and encouraging inward investment. This tried and tested approach not only benefits the country as a whole, but also trickles down to private businesses and even individuals seeking a career in the space industry. By capturing the imagination of the public, the UAE's focus soon shifted to manned space exploration and sending Emiratis into space.

# CHAPTER 6

## THE FIRST UAE ASTRONAUTS

Space programs often capture the imagination of the public, and sending probes to other planets can push scientists to the forefront. Beautiful images of faraway galaxies and black holes gain shares on social media and reveal the beauty of the universe. However, drawing upon the instinctual need of humanity to explore, manned space missions create a certain romance and excitement.

Even now, we devour grainy black and white videos of Armstrong's first steps on the moon, and talk about pioneers like Yuri Gagarin and John Glenn. While developing a space program can appeal to the public, sending astronauts into space resonates and also inspires others. Accordingly, after the progress with establishing its aerospace industry, the thoughts of the UAE's leaders and scientists now turned towards sending Emiratis into space.

Crossing this boundary would not only provide the natural cumulation of decades of work towards this point, it would unite Emiratis and other Arabs behind the program. Importantly, astronauts soon become national heroes and would inspire young Emiratis to see the space program as a career.

Not only would this produce the astronauts of the future, but it would encourage young people across the Arab world to learn the skills they need to help the country become the leading aerospace hub in the region. By building partnerships with other space agencies and participating in rigorous selection programs, the UAE was ready to find the right people to send into space, carrying the hopes of an entire nation.

## UAE Astronaut Training Program

Becoming an astronaut is something that very few people can do, because it is one of the most physically, mentally, and psychological challenging jobs possible. Astronauts need to be intelligent, physically fit, and with the ability to remain calm under pressure.

Due to these high physical and mental requirements, picking the right people was crucial and the UAE needed a tough selection process to find the best candidates. Not only did they need to excel and possess the ability to learn quickly, they also needed charisma to engage with Emiratis draw attention to the program.

In 2017, the UAE established the United Arab Emirates' Astronaut Program as the natural next step of its space program. After a series of satellite designs and launches, manned exploration of space signified the next step that would establish the UAE as a truly spacefaring nation. [90]

As a carefully designed program that drew from long-established practices elsewhere, the UAE Astronaut Training Program gives Emiratis the skills they need to participate in manned space missions. Administered by the Mohammed bin Rashid Space Centre (MBRSC), the program set out to find the perfect candidates before setting them on a robust and comprehensive training and preparation program. Crucially, the program needed to produce astronauts with

---

[90] UAE Astronaut Program, *MBRSC*, https://www.mbrsc.ae/service/astronaut_prog/

all of the skills and abilities needed to partake in international space missions.

The UAE understood that crossing this boundary and sending astronauts into space would inspire the next generation of Emirati scientists and engineers far more than the satellite programs. There is always a romance about sending people into space, and the MRBSC hoped the program would inspire young Emiratis and encourage them to study STEM subjects. [91]

In addition, while developing technical and scientific expertise is important for a space program, the publicity of a manned mission captures attention in the UAE and also internationally, signifying the country is now a major player in the space industry.[92,93] With the program in place, the next step involved assessing over 4,000 applications to find the perfect people.[94]

## The Selection Process

Keen to find the best candidates, the MBRSC set up an extremely rigorous astronaut selection program intended to help them sift through the thousands of candidates. Using a number of tests and evaluations, the program looked for only the potential

---

[91] UAE Astronaut Program, *MBRSC*, https://www.mbrsc.ae/service/astronaut_prog/

[92] UAE Astronaut Program, *MBRSC*, https://www.mbrsc.ae/service/astronaut_prog

[93] Saseendran, Sajila, How UAE's Astronaut Programme demonstrates country's boundless ambitions, *Gulf News*, February 23, 2023, https://gulfnews.com/uae/how-uaes-astronaut-programme-demonstrates-countrys-boundless-ambitions-1.94038518

[94] Over 4000 Emiratis Volunteer for UAE Astronaut Selection, *Spacewatch Middle East*, April 2018, https://spacewatch.global/2018/04/4000-emiratis-volunteer-uae-astronaut-selection/

candidates fitting the most physical, mental, and psychological criteria.

Applications came from a number of fields, including pilots, engineers, and scientists, giving a broad range of skills and experience to choose from. Gradually, the program delivered a shortlist of people ready to move to the next stage and begin training.

Once selected, the candidates embarked upon an intensive training program that encompassed the huge body of knowledge they would need to function efficiently and safely in orbit. Candidates learned a range of technical skills, including space science, engineering, mechanics, spacecraft systems, and the extremely important safety and survival training. [95]

## The Training Program

Drawing from its experiences with the entire national aerospace development, the MSRBC knew that partnering with external organizations and tapping into their knowledge made sense. Accordingly, they often conducted training alongside other agencies including NASA, the European Space Agency (ESA), and Russia's Roscosmos. [96]

Because most missions were likely to include the International Space Station, the astronauts received training in ISS systems and

---

[95] Soaring Beyond The Skies: A Deep Dive Into The UAE's Astronaut Programs, *New Space Economy,* July 25, 2023, https://newspaceeconomy.ca/2023/07/25/soaring-beyond-the-skies-a-deep-dive-into-the-uaes-astronaut-program-56192/
[96] Soaring Beyond The Skies: A Deep Dive Into The UAE's Astronaut Programs, *New Space Economy,* July 25, 2023, https://newspaceeconomy.ca/2023/07/25/soaring-beyond-the-skies-a-deep-dive-into-the-uaes-astronaut-program-56192/

operations, as well as the ongoing scientific research. Other training covered extravehicular activity (EVA) and robotics, ensuring that the astronauts would be able to operate outside the ISS and use the robotic arms needed to perform maintenance and support spacewalks and docking.[97] [98]

While theory is important in space, practical experience is crucial, so the UAE's potential astronauts engaged in simulated mission training. This covered normal operations during spaceflights and the ISS, but also provided valuable experience in dealing with emergency situations, operating in microgravity, and conducting experiments within the confines of the space station. [99]

## Announcing the First Astronauts

After the selection process and the initial training, the MSRBC was now confident that it had a pool of trainees with the right skills and experiences to undertake space missions. In September 2018, the UAE announced its first two astronauts, Hazza Ali Mansouri and Sultan Al Neyadi. Determined to succeed, they trained together, preparing themselves for the difficult missions that lay ahead.

*HAZZA ALI MANSOURI*

---

[97] ESA, *European Robotic Arm*,
https://www.esa.int/Science_Exploration/Human_and_Robotic_Exploration/International
_Space_Station/European_Robotic_Arm
[98] Soaring Beyond The Skies: A Deep Dive Into The UAE's Astronaut Programs, *New Space Economy,* July 25, 2023, https://newspaceeconomy.ca/2023/07/25/soaring-beyond-the-skies-a-deep-dive-into-the-uaes-astronaut-program-56192/
[99] Soaring Beyond The Skies: A Deep Dive Into The UAE's Astronaut Programs, *New Space Economy,* July 25, 2023, https://newspaceeconomy.ca/2023/07/25/soaring-beyond-the-skies-a-deep-dive-into-the-uaes-astronaut-program-56192/

After his long training program, in 2019, Hazza Ali Mansouri became the first Emirati to go onto space. He spent eight days aboard the ISS, conducting scientific experiments and reaching out to Emirati children and students. This journey proved a significant moment for the UAE's space program and showed that the country was serious about carving its place in the space program.

His flight, dubbed 'Zayed's Ambition,' made the UAE the 19th country to send an astronaut to the ISS and the first Arab nation to do so. He also became the backup astronaut for Sultan Al Neyadi's mission in 2023. He became the first Arab leader of an ISS expedition during this mission.[100, 101] Al Mansouri quickly became a national hero, capturing the imagination of Emiratis and earning his place in history.

*SULTAN AL NEYADI*

Although he had to wait longer, especially in a world restricted by a pandemic, in 2023, Sultan Al Neyadi became the second Emirati astronaut to enter orbit. He made history as the first Arab astronaut to embark on a six-month mission to the International Space Station (ISS) as part of Expedition 69. Additionally, he achieved the distinction of being the first Arab astronaut to conduct a spacewalk. Prior to his groundbreaking mission, Al Neyadi served as the backup astronaut for Hazza Al Mansouri during the UAE's inaugural scientific expedition to the ISS in 2019. On March 2, 2023, Al Neyadi and his NASA SpaceX Crew-6 team were launched from Cape Canaveral in Florida. Notably, Al Neyadi accomplished the

---

[100] UAE Astronaut Program, *MBRSC,* https://www.mbrsc.ae/service/astronaut_prog
[101] Hazzan Ali Mansouri, *MBRSC,* https://www.mbrsc.ae/team/hazzaa_ali_almansoori/

remarkable feat of becoming the first Arab astronaut to participate in a spacewalk during Expedition 69, partnering with NASA astronaut Stephen Bowen. Their spacewalk, lasting 7 hours and 1 minute, included a series of critical tasks such as the installation of power cables in preparation for the iROSA installation.

## The Next Group

In 2021, the next astronauts emerged from the UAE's rigorous astronaut training program, namely Nora Al Matrooshi and Mohammad Al Mulla. By naming Al Matrooshi in its group, the UAE signaled its intention to send the first female Arab astronaut into space. By doing this, the country showed how it intends to inspire young Emirati women to follow careers in science, engineering, and technology.

### *NORA AL MATROOSHI*

Selected for the second group of UAE astronaut trainees, Nora Al Matrooshi became the first female Arab astronaut trainee. She entered NASA's astronaut candidate class of 2021 and underwent intensive training in the US. Training alongside Mohammad Al Mulla at the Johnson Space Center in Houston, Al Matrooshi is preparing for spaceflights and missions to the ISS.

The intensive training covers time in a centrifuge and scuba diving to give them these determined Emirate astronauts the skills they will need. On this course, Al Matrooshi refined her skillset and learned a range of survival skills as part of the two-year astronaut training program that began in January 2022.[102,103]

Nora Al Matrooshi wanted to be an astronaut from a very young age and often dreamed of taking spaceflights to the moon, letting her imagination explore the wonders of the universe. This vision shaped her path through life and she eventually took a degree in mechanical engineering at the United Arab Emirates University. Although she never believed that she would ever have the opportunity, Al Matrooshi wanted to make sure she had the right skills for becoming an astronaut. The young Nora could not have possibly imagined that, years later, her dreams would come to fruition when she was selected for the program.[104]

With women representing only 1 in 10 of astronauts, Nora Al Matrooshi is a trailblazer not just for Arab women but for women everywhere. Now, NASA intends to land a woman on the moon in the next few years through its Artemis program, and a third of the applicants for the second MBRSC program were women. Nora continues to meet students in the UAE and shows them how they can achieve their dreams, becoming a role model for many.

## *MOHAMMED AL MULLA*

Mohammed Al Mulla is a skilled helicopter pilot with experience of working for the police. He believes that his training provides him with some of the spatial skill and reactions needed to be an astronaut.

---

[102] Nora Al Matrooshi, *MBRSC,* https://www.mbrsc.ae/team/nora/

[103] Mohammed Al Mulla, *MBRSA,* https://www.mbrsc.ae/team/mohammed_mulla/

[104] Khogeer, Khadijah, Exclusive: The UAE's First Female Astronaut, Nora Al Matrooshi, Is Exploring A New Frontier For Arab Women In Space, *Forbes,* March 11, 2022, https://www.forbesmiddleeast.com/leadership/women-leaders/interview

As a helicopter pilot, he has had to deal with emergencies and understands the need for following procedures.

A native of Dubai, Al Mulla received a commercial license when he was only, making him the police force's youngest pilot. Now 33, he trains other pilots for the Dubai Police Department and has also received decorations for bravery. His ambition is to become part of the first Emirati team to set foot on the moon, and like all of the other Emirati astronauts, is proud to represent his country as its space program develops.[105]

## Building Links with International Space Agencies

Throughout its astronaut training, the MBRSC worked closely with other international agencies, especially NASA. By doing this, the UAE can use their expertise and also ensure that their astronauts are potential candidates for selection on a number of missions. Due to the level of international cooperation in space, these partnerships will prove crucial to the development of the UAE's space program.

## Cooperation with NASA

The UAE's astronauts join NASA's Astronaut Candidate Selection (ASCAN), which makes them eligible for most space missions when they graduate. This includes missions to the ISS, but also covers commercial company launches, and the UAE is discussing

---

[105] Nasir, Sarwhat, Dubai Police pilot turned astronaut sets sights on the Moon, *The National,* July 7, 2021, https://www.thenationalnews.com/uae/2021/07/07/dubai-police-pilot-turned-astronaut-sets-sights-on-the-moon/

participation in the Artemis program with NASA, which will seek to develop permanent bases on the moon. [106]

As part of the selection process, the UAE's trainee astronauts learn Russian, the ISS systems, and robotics. The program also includes leadership training, learning how to fly T-38 jets, and performing spacewalks. The UAE's whole program is supported by a Reimbursable Space Act Agreement between NASA and the MBRSC, which gives the country's astronauts access to the training program and facilities. [107]

In 2018, the UAE's space agency and NASA signed an agreement covering manned spaceflight, including the potential Gateway program to create a space station orbiting the Moon. NASA is already preparing for closing down the ISS at the end of the decade and Gateway could replace it as a science laboratory. Through the agreement, the UAE has an opportunity to be at the heart of this, potentially including Emirati astronauts. [108]

## Cooperation with the ESA, Roscosmos, and SpaceX

[106] Nasir, Sarwat, UAE's new astronauts to begin Nasa's two-year training programme in Houston, *The National,* December 5, 2021, https://www.thenationalnews.com/uae/2021/11/21/uaes-new-astronauts-to-begin-nasas-2-year-training-programme-in-houston/

[107] Nasa to train Emirati astronauts for long-haul space missions, *Dubai Air Show,* September 23, 2020, https://www.dubaiairshow.aero/nasa-train-emirati-astronauts-long-haul-space-missions

[108] Nasir, Sarwat, UAE's new astronauts to begin Nasa's two-year training programme in Houston, *The National,* December 5, 2021, https://www.thenationalnews.com/uae/2021/11/21/uaes-new-astronauts-to-begin-nasas-2-year-training-programme-in-houston/

Along with its strong partnership with NASA, the UAE is working with other agencies, including the European Space Agency (ESA) and Roscosmos. The first Emirati astronauts underwent training at the ESA Columbus training module for the SpaceX Crew 6 mission, covering theoretical and practical aspects.

To supplement this, the astronauts received additional the training at the European Astronaut Training Centre (EAC), in Cologne, Germany, which covers all European-designed hardware used in the ISS. At this advanced center, the astronauts learned about maintenance, hardware, and maintenance of the station.[109]

For Al Mansouri's mission, the UAE worked with Roscosmos to learn the skills needed for launch on a Soyuz rocket.[110] For the later Axiom mission, Al Neyadi also trained at the Johnson Space Center, SpaceX headquarters in California, and in Florida.[111]

**Providing Inspiration**

After the missions, the UAE's astronauts engaged in educational outreach and public appearances intended to help kindle the spark of exploration and hunger for knowledge within young Emiratis. The

[109] UAE astronauts complete key phase of training for SpaceX Crew 6 mission, *The National,* December 17, 2022, https://www.thenationalnews.com/uae/uae-in-space/2022/12/17/uae-astronauts-complete-key-phase-of-training-for-spacex-crew-6-mission/

[110] UAE astronauts complete key phase of training for SpaceX Crew 6 mission, *The National,* December 17, 2022, https://www.thenationalnews.com/uae/uae-in-space/2022/12/17/uae-astronauts-complete-key-phase-of-training-for-spacex-crew-6-mission/

[111] UAE astronauts complete key phase of training for SpaceX Crew 6 mission, *The National,* December 17, 2022, https://www.thenationalnews.com/uae/uae-in-space/2022/12/17/uae-astronauts-complete-key-phase-of-training-for-spacex-crew-6-mission/

UAE's astronaut program is helping to inspire future generations of engineers, scientists, and astronauts, helping the country to develop its knowledge-based economy and investing for the future.[112]

By raising the profile of the UAE and showing that it is willing and able to participate in space, the country will be able to attract interest and investment in its growing aerospace sector and wider economy, placing it as a leader in the Arab world and a global leader.

Ultimately, amid the conflicts on earth and fractious relationships, space is one area where countries still work together for a common good. By actively participating, the UAE is helping to develop a global community that promotes human progress and scientific endeavor.

Going forward, the UAE's astronaut program will continue to develop and train astronauts and actively participate in future space missions. The training program will cover the skills needed for any planned missions to the Moon and Mars, making sure that the country's astronauts and ground crews can work with country's ambitions for extraterrestrial exploration. Importantly, this development will build upon collaborations with other space agencies, sharing knowledge and expertise and working towards common goals.

## Find The Right People And Let Them Inspire Others

The space race between the US and Russia saw humans go from sending satellites into space to flights by intrepid cosmonauts and

---

[112] UAE Astronauts Inspire Next Generation of Space Explorers, *Gulf News,* January 9, 2023, https://www.pressreader.com/uae/gulf-news/20230109/281599539595336

astronauts in just a few years. These missions captured the eyes of the world's media, making Gagarin, Glenn, Armstrong, and Tereshkova into household names. These people represented the best humanity had to offer, as intelligent, skilled, and courageous astronauts driven to make history and advance human knowledge.

Now, while it is easier for people to fly into space, with better technology, more space agencies, and commercial flights, the requirements for astronauts are as stringent as ever. In some ways, given the wealth of new equipment and new technologies on modern spacecraft and the ISS, astronauts need to be exceptional and able to learn quickly.

For this reason, the UAE developed a stringent astronaut selection program to make sure that it could find the best candidates and maximize the chances of success. In addition, by working with other space agencies and training facilities, the MRSBC could ensure that all its astronauts receive the best-in-class training and are ready to undertake any mission.

With the first missions undertaken, the country's astronauts are now also important communicators, sharing their experiences. They tirelessly reach out to schools, universities, and young Arabs everywhere, providing a source of inspiration for those wanting to work in the space industry. The astronauts are normal Emiratis who worked hard to achieve success and show others that it is possible to follow dreams. The UAE's astronauts will continue to be a source of inspiration for decades to come and show how finding the right people can be the most important investment of all.

# CHAPTER 7

## THE SPACE MISSION BEGINS

As an entire country waited, the countdown began as a Soyuz MS-15 spacecraft readied for launch on the Gagarin pad at the Baikonur Cosmodrome. This site was steeped in history, as the launch site for Sputnik, the first satellite that ignited the space race. From here, the iconic Vostok spacecraft that sent the great Yuri Gagarin into orbit launched as one of the defining moments of the 20th Century.

Now, as the last scheduled mission from this iconic launchpad, another page of history was written. As the countdown progressed, Emiratis watched one of their own, praying and hoping as he represented their country and its ambitions for space. As the Soyuz left the pad, slowly but inexorably screaming into the sky, the tension released as the launch went without any problems.

On September 25, 2019, Hazza Al Mansouri became the first Emirati astronaut to travel to space, onboard Soyuz MS-15 spacecraft. He spent eight days on the International Space Station, conducting experiments and sharing his experiences with people back on Earth.[113]

His story of how he relentlessly followed his dreams shows how a young Emirati who grew up near the trackless dunes of the Empty

---

[113] Final Soyuz-FG rocket delivers ISS crew, *Russian Space Web,* https://www.russianspaceweb.com/soyuz-ms-15.html

Quarter could become the symbol for the UAE's space program and ambitions. Just a few years later, Sultan Al Neyadi completed the first Arab Space Walk from the ISS and showed that the UAE is in space for the long haul.

## Early Life and Career

As the first Emirati, and one of the first Arabs in space, Hazza Al Mansouri's journey inspired generations but was also the culmination of a life and career spent working towards that moment. Born on the 13th December, 1983, in Abu Dhabi, one can imagine that Hazza spent his early years exploring the desert of Liwa, looking to the stars and meteors in the clear skies setting out the path he wanted to take in life.

Living on the edge of the Empty Quarter, he had a view of the night skies uninterrupted by light pollution, and this may have kindled his passion for travelling into space. Once he graduated from school, his love of the stars steered him towards a degree in aviation at the Khalifa bin Zayed Air College.[114]

While his dream of becoming an astronaut never went away, he took the opportunity to join the air force and become a pilot, content to explain the stars and universe to his children while gazing upon the desert skies.

His prowess led him to becoming a Functional Check Flight (FCF) Pilot F-16B60, which involved a three-year program in

---

[114] Degl'Innocenti, Francesco, 50u: Interview With Hazzaa Al-Mansoori, The First Emirati In Space, *Archis*, May 13, 2022, https://archis.org/volume/50u-interview-with-hazzaa-al-mansoori-the-first-emirati-in-space

Arizona. Four years after returning to the UAE, he became the youngest military F-16 pilot and continued to develop his career as one of the leading pilots in the UAE. His life changed when Sheikh Mohammed bin Rashid ask for people to apply to become astronauts, and applied, hoping that his skills as a pilot would prove useful. They did, and Hazza became one of the first group of astronauts selected.

In the final stages of the selection process, Hazza travelled to Russia for the final stages of the selection process, alongside nine other candidates.

## Astronaut Training

As part of his training, Hazza was selected from over 4,000 candidates after a series of exhaustive tests in the UAE and abroad. The fitness and skills he had acquired as a jet pilot stood him in good stead mentally and physically, and he already possessed many of the necessary skills. He had quick reactions, knew how to follow procedures to the letter, and understood how communicate with other members of the crew.

As part of an agreement between Roscosmos and MBRSC over the training of Emirati astronauts, Hazza underwent training at the Yuri Gagarin Training Center in Star City, Russia. This gave him the skills and experience he would need for the ISS. The other courses he took included survival, spatial disorientation, and many others essential skills.

Hazza and his colleague, Sultan Al Neyadi, also had to spend a year learning Russian to make sure that he could understand the rest of his team and follow all instructions and procedures.[115] Training also took place with NASA in Houston and the ESA in Cologne, while the UAE also has training agreements with the Japan Aerospace Exploration Agency (JAXA).

In April 2019, the MBRSC announced that Hazza Al Mansouri would be the chosen astronaut for an eight-day mission to the ISS on Soyuz MS-15, returning on Soyuz MS-12. On the 25th September, 2019, Hazza launched from the Baikonur Cosmodrome and spent six hours in free flight in space before docking with the ISS.

Training for the ISS included training for all modules and sections of the station. The astronauts learned how to use all of its equipment and what to do in an emergency such as fire or pressure drop. They also underwent survival training to help them survive the capsule landed in a remote area of sea or land. Overall, he underwent almost 100 different courses and put in almost 1,500 hours of total training.[116]

Al Mansouri learned how to move in a spacesuit under zero gravity. He also learned skills such as using the camera, performing tasks such as cooking and cleaning, communicating with the ground, and taking photos of the planet stretched below. All of this would

---

[115] Ryan, Patrick, Hazza Al Mansouri on being mobbed at the mosque and inspiring the next generation, *The National UAE*, November 5, 2019, https://www.thenationalnews.com/uae/hazza-al-mansouri-on-being-mobbed-at-the-mosque-and-inspiring-the-next-generation-1.933147

[116] UAE Astronaut Programme: A track record of scientific discovery, *WAM*, September 3, 2023, https://wam.ae/en/details/1395303192103

ensure he was a valuable member of the team, contributing to the mission. [117]

## Blast Off

Before the launch, Hazza sent out a Tweet laying out his feelings and his pride at taking this step for his country:[118]

*"A few hours before launch and I'm filled with this indescribable feeling of glory and awe. Today I carry the dreams and ambition of my country to a whole new dimension. May Allah grant me success in this mission. Your brother, Hazzaa AlMansoori."*

After a cancelled launch, Hazza Al Mansouri and his team launched on Wednesday, 25th September 2019, carrying the hopes and dreams of his country. Live streamed on Arab news channels and social media, this became a defining moment in Emirati history with the country almost coming to a standstill as people watched, praying for a safe journey.

UAE President Sheikh Mohamed bin Zayed Al Nahyan, then Crown Prince of Abu Dhabi, expressed the significance of the mission:[119]

*"I proudly watched as Hazza Al Mansouri lifted off into space. This event strengthens our confidence in our youth who will take our nation*

---

[117] ESA expertise aids UAE spaceflight, *European Space Agency,* September 18, 2019, https://www.esa.int/Science_Exploration/Human_and_Robotic_Exploration/ESA_experti se_aids_UAE_spaceflight

[118] Hazza Al Mansouri, Personal Tweet, https://twitter.com/astro_hazzaa/status/1176821479264141314

[119] Sheikh Mohamed Bin Zayed, Personal Tweet, https://twitter.com/MohamedBinZayed/status/1176864571983826945

*to new heights and reinforces our ambitions for the future. We pray for Hazza's success and his safe return home."*

With Oleg Skrpochka, the mission leader, and an American, Jessica Meir, they reached the ISS after a six-hour journey. After a short delay, the Soyuz docked and Hazza was ready to begin his mission.

## Into the Mission and Returning Home

Once aboard the ISS, Al Mansouri performed 15 experiments suggested by Emirati school students as part of the MBRSC 'Science in Space' competition. This experiment, in conjunction with NanoRocks, a company from Houston, selected 32 experiments from Emirati students to test the effects of weightlessness on various substances. Other experiments included studying oil emulsification and trying to germinate a date palm seed native to the region.[120]

Hazza also gave the first tour of the ISS in the Arabic language and performed a number of earth observation experiments. On the 3rd October 2019, Al Mansouri stepped onto the Soyuz 12 spacecraft ready for the return to Earth. After five hours of free flight, they eventually reentered the atmosphere and landed on the open steppes of Kazakhstan, where he returned to Star City before a flight home.

---

[120] Chang, Kenneth, Hazzaa al-Mansoori, First U.A.E. Astronaut, Launches to Space Station, *New York Times,* September 25, 2019,
https://www.nytimes.com/2019/09/25/science/emirati-astronaut-uae-international-space-station.html

There, in front of the media, he entered national folklore as a hero. [121]

## Legacy

Since his return to the UAE, Hazza has worked tirelessly to share his experiences and support his country's growing space industry. He is always willing to engage with people and talk about his experiences, showing young Emiratis that they can become part of the growing dream to make the nation a growing influence in space.

Al Mansouri is happy to compare the growth of the UAE's space industry with the successes of the US and Russia in opening up space for exploration. He is passionate in his belief that the country can break boundaries and that astronauts in the UAE and nearby countries can appeal to young Arabs and encourage them to follow his path.

Hazza believes that his journey has sparked interest in young Arabs, with crowds of children wanting to meet him and talk about his experiences. Hopefully, these will become the astronauts, engineers, and scientists that will propel the UAE and Arab regions into space.

He was proud of achieving Sheikh Zayed's space ambition dreamt up decades ago and sees it as a beginning rather than a final destination. Importantly, he learned on the ISS that humanity can

---

[121] Here's What The First Emirati Astronaut, Hazza Al Mansouri, Experienced In Space, *GQ Middle East,* September 25, 2019, https://www.gqmiddleeast.com/culture/eight-days-in-space

achieve great things when people work together towards common goals. [122]

Since his first mission, Al Mansouri has continued to train, with a year of training in NASA's Johnson Space Center, and he soon became qualified to work as an ISS operator. Other qualifications include using the Extravehicular Mobility Unit, learning how to rescue incapacitated crew, and understanding how to maintain the ISS. [123]

Ready for more missions, he is now an experienced astronaut with all the skills needed to contribute to international space programs. Hazza served as back up and mission support for Sultan Al Neyadi's 2023 mission into space.

## NASA's SpaceX Crew 6 mission

In 2022, the UAE and Axiom Space signed an agreement to fly an Emirati crew member to the ISS on NASA's SpaceX Crew 6 mission. Sultan Al Neyadi joined the crew of four as a mission specialist performing experiments in the ISS' microgravity laboratory,

---

[122] Ryan, Patrick, Hazza Al Mansouri on being mobbed at the mosque and inspiring the next generation, *The National UAE,* November 5, 2019,
https://www.thenationalnews.com/uae/hazza-al-mansouri-on-being-mobbed-at-the-mosque-and-inspiring-the-next-generation-1.933147
[123] Sarwat, Nasir, UAE astronauts in line for spacewalks after completing first year of training at NASA, *The National,* October 8, 2021,
https://www.thenationalnews.com/uae/uae-in-space/2021/10/08/uae-astronauts-in-line-for-spacewalks-after-completing-first-year-of-training-at-nasa/

demonstrating technology, and performing routine maintenance activities. [124]

The international crew flew on a SpaceX Dragon Endeavour spacecraft with a Falcon 9 booster, lifting off from NASA's Kennedy Space Center in Florida. Alongside NASA astronauts Stephen Bowen, the mission commander, and Woody Hoburg, the pilot, Sultan Al Neyadi joined cosmonaut Andrey Fedyaev as a mission specialist. On March 23rd, 2023, the Endeavour docked with the ISS at 1.40am EST while over the Indian Ocean.

Docking was delayed by a faulty docking hook sensor on Endeavour, which needed troubleshooting and a software override. Soon, after leak checks and pressurization, the Endeavor opened its hatches and Sultan join the rest of the team, taking his first steps onto the ISS. [125]

Six months later Sultan Al Neyadi and his comrades successfully splashed down in the Atlantic Ocean just off the coast of Florida. In his time aboard the ISS, Sultan completed almost 6,000 earth orbits and 79 million miles. During his six months, Sultan performed over

---

[124] Soaring Beyond The Skies: A Deep Dive Into The UAE's Astronaut Programs, *New Space Economy,* July 25, 2023, https://newspaceeconomy.ca/2023/07/25/soaring-beyond-the-skies-a-deep-dive-into-the-uaes-astronaut-program-56192/
[125] Garcia, Mark, SpaceX Crew-6 Mission Docks to Station's Harmony Module, *NASA,* March 3, 2023, https://blogs.nasa.gov/commercialcrew/2023/03/03/spacex-crew-6-mission-docks-to-stations-harmony-module/

2,000 scientific experiments, conducted several spacewalks, upgraded the ISS' power systems, and installed new solar arrays. [126, 127]

Across the UAE, schools and workplaces broadcast the mission as the nation watched on. UAE President Sheikh Mohamed bin Zayed Al Nahyan announced:

*"The participation of Emiratis in this mission is seen as a step closer towards achieving our vision of ensuring a better future for generations and strengthen their participation in building the future."* [128]

Hamad Obaid Al Mansoori, chairman of MBRSC announced:

*"As we venture into the depths of space, we carry with us the hopes and dreams of our nation, and the determination to make history. Today, we celebrate not just the successful launch of the longest Arab space mission in history, but the realization of a vision that will inspire generations to come."*

*"We are highly grateful of our wise leadership whose constant support is a source of strength and inspiration for the team to constantly take on new challenges. Our mission through these scientific endeavors is to keep the UAE flag flying high and be at the forefront of countries contributing to scientific achievements."*

---

[126] Lewis, Russell, Splashdown! NASA's Crew-6 returns after 6 months at the International Space Station, *NPR,* September 4, 2023, https://www.npr.org/2023/09/04/1197481976/spacex-nasa-crew-6-iss-returns-earth-splashdown

[127] Sultan Saif Al Neyadi, *MBRSC,* https://www.mbrsc.ae/team/sultan_saif/

[128] *Middle East Economy,* UAE President, Dubai Ruler praises successful launch of UAE space mission, May 29, 2023, https://economymiddleeast.com/news/uae-president-dubai-ruler-praises-successful-launch-of-uae-space-mission/

Salem al-Marri, Director General of MBRSC, noted how the mission showed that the UAE was serious about its space program.[129] Like Hazza, Sultan is also a believer than missions like his inspire younger generations and can help the UAE develop a leading space industry and encourage the scientists of the future. [130]

During the flight, Sultan posted numerous updates of life aboard the ISS on his social media, in Arabic, and believed that that people across the Middle East and North Africa wanted to learn much more about space. By providing information, he hoped to act as a source of inspiration for the region. [131]

## Always Look to The Future

The flights of Hazza Al Mansouri and Sultan Al Neyadi captured the imagination of the public globally and also announced to the world that the country is serious about its space program. For its space program and aviation industry, the UAE intends to remain at the forefront of adopting new technologies and approaches.

With its intention of sending missions to the Moon and to Mars, as well as continuing to design and sent satellites into orbit.

---

[129] Jennifer Bell, UAE's historic space mission: SpaceX astronauts blast off, Al Arabiya News, March 2, 2022, https://english.alarabiya.net/News/gulf/2023/03/02/UAE-s-historic-space-mission-SpaceX-astronauts-ready-for-blast-off-

[130] Ryan, Patrick, Hazza Al Mansouri on being mobbed at the mosque and inspiring the next generation, *The National UAE,* November 5, 2019, https://www.thenationalnews.com/uae/hazza-al-mansouri-on-being-mobbed-at-the-mosque-and-inspiring-the-next-generation-1.933147

[131] Holmes, Oliver, 'A big responsibility': astronaut from UAE on longest ever Arab space mission, *The Guardian,* September 1, 2023, https://www.theguardian.com/science/2023/sep/01/astronaut-uae-arab-world-space-sultan-al-neyadi

By continuing to invest in people, build lasting partnerships, and embrace new technologies, the future remains optimistic and in line with the vision of Sheikh Zayed bin Sultan Al Nahyan.

# CHAPTER 8

## THE FUTURE OF THE UAE'S AVIATION AND SPACE INDUSTRIES

The successful culmination of the UAE's astronaut program was a landmark that heralded the arrival of the country as a spacefaring nation. It showed exactly how far the UAE's aviation and space industries have come since the founding of Emirates Airlines.

The country's ambitious vision for space exploration, coupled with its investment in infrastructure and education, position it as a leader in these industries. As always, the UAE does not intend to remain content and is already planning ahead, looking at how the aerospace industry can help the country develop and benefit ordinary citizens. Rather than a final goal, the UAE's aviation and space industries will touch every aspect of society and act as a starting point for societal and economic change.

## People and Culture

Often overlooked in favor of science and technology, the UAE's successes in aerospace and the space program have profound effects on its people and culture. The country has transformed in recent decades, embracing science and technology while building some of the most modern infrastructure in the world.

Now, the people of the country are also changing and want to be part of the process, seeking new careers in its growing high-technology sector and following paths thought impossible just a couple of generations ago. One important foundation of the program is the growing role of women, who are now taking their rightful place and becoming the scientists, astronauts, and engineers of the future.

## The Role of Women

The UAE has ensured that women play a prominent role in its space program because the country understands the importance of engaging with all Emiratis. The country's young population is increasingly well-educated and well-motivated, and it is important to make sure that the best students have opportunities without separating them by gender.

Training a female astronaut creates publicity and appeals to women in the country, encouraging them to study engineering, project management, science, technology, and all other skills needed by any program. Now, women are prominent at all levels of the aerospace program, from designing and building satellites to running missions and taking positions of political responsibility.

Over a third of the astronaut candidates were women, and the UAE employs women at every level of its aviation and space programs. 50% of employees at the UAESA are women, including Sarah Al Amiri, UAE Minister of State for Public Education and Advanced Technology, and Heyam Al Blooshi, a UAE Space Agency engineer who worked on the Hope Probe.[132,133]

---

[132] UAE Space Exploration, *UAE USA United,* https://www.uaeusaunited.com/stories/uae-space-exploration

[133] Malek, Caline, Emirati has sights on UAE mission to Mars, *The National,* July 10, 2015, https://www.thenationalnews.com/uae/emirati-has-sights-on-uae-mission-to-mars-1.32003

## *SARAH AL AMIRI AND THE MARS MISSION*

One notable program with a high participation of women is the UAE's Mars Program, which made the country the fifth to reach the planet and the first Arab interplanetary mission. The mission, costing over $200 million, launched the Hope Probe from Japan. It is currrently sending data concerning the Martian atmosphere and climate to reveal more secrets about Earth's nearest neighbor.

As Minister of State for Space, Sarah Al Amiri played a prominent role in developing and overseeing the program. Notably, women made up the majority of the Mars Mission team, with Al Amiri pointing out that 80% of the science team are women. They were selected on merit and according to what skills they would contribute towards the success of the mission. This is part of Al Amiri's belief that traditional gender expectations should not affect the UAE's approach to its space program and to science in general.[134] [135]

Sarah already serves as Minister of State for Science, working closely with the Hope Mission, a passion of hers. [136] She was also appointed as Chairwoman of the United Arab Emirates Space Agency (UAESA).

---

[134] UAE Women Lead Arab World's First Mars Mission, *DW*, February 9, 2021, https://www.dw.com/en/uae-women-scientists-lead-arab-worlds-first-space-mission-to-mars/a-56513724

[135] AlShuwaihi, Hessa, Beyond the Glass Ceiling: UAE Women Propelling Space Science Forward, *UAE Embassy*, March 28, 2023, https://www.uae-embassy.org/news/beyond-glass-ceiling-uae-women-propelling-space-science-forward

[136] Kluger, Jeffrey, Sarah Al Amiri: The Woman Who Took the U.A.E. to Mars, *TIME*, February 24, 2022, https://time.com/6150593/sarah-al-amiri-mars/

Sarah created, as Minister of State for Advanced Technology, a team to encourage more women to seek a career in science with prospects for advancement as she herself progressed. Her own ascent shows other women that they can follow their ambitions and thrive.[137]

## The Growing Influence of Women in the Space Sector

At present, women make up 45% of the space sector workforce in the UAE, far exceeding the 12% average for other space agencies. It is a sign of the country's active policies intended to open up career paths for women in science and ensure that Emirati women represent their country internationally.

In the UAE, women are involved in all aspects of the space sector, from research and manufacturing satellites to running departments and even preparing to go into space. The UAE's leaders point out that this is part of a wider program to increase the representation of women in all sectors as part of a shift towards empowerment and equality.

Emirati women worked on all aspects of the KhalifaSat, the Hope Probe, and all other aspects of the country's space program. Now, Emirati women are working for NASA and the ESA and entering training programs Many want to be part of exploring space as well as helping their country tackle issues such as water shortages and climate change.[138]

---

[137] Kluger, Jeffrey, Sarah Al Amiri: The Woman Who Took the U.A.E. to Mars, *TIME,* February 24, 2022, https://time.com/6150593/sarah-al-amiri-mars/

[138] Emirati women take lead in UAE space sector, *Aviation Guide,* https://aviationguideem.com/emirati-women-take-lead-in-uae-space-sector/

## A Youthful Workforce

Reflecting the young population of the UAE and the MENA region in general, educating young Emiratis is a core objective of the UAE's space program. For example, the average age of people involved in the Hope Probe was under 35, while schemes such as the Mini Satellite Challenge were other ways to engage youth.[139]

A number of other programs encourage youth to pursue careers within the space program, such as the 'Like a Scientist' camps and ambassador programs for teachers.[140] These ideas all work alongside the publicity generated by the space program and the Emirati astronauts to spark interest and make STEM subjects interesting.

## The Arab Space Pioneers Program

One prominent program is the Arab Space Pioneers Program, designed to fast track young Arabs into the space program. It is the first science training scheme of its type in the region and selected seven candidates from over 37,000 applicants to train with experts. The successful candidates learn about a range of subjects including robotics, space engineering, space entrepreneurship, artificial intelligence, and a number of other specialties.

With support from the American Space Foundation, the program provides an educational gateway and creates opportunities. Started in July 2020, the program drew upon the publicity from the

---

[139] 10 Things You Should Know About the UAE Space Program, 2019

[140] Nasir, Sarwat, Emirati women are playing a central role in UAE's space sector, *The National,* August 28, 2020, https://www.thenationalnews.com/uae/science/emirati-women-are-playing-a-central-role-in-uae-s-space-sector-1.1069667

UAE's Mars Mission and is intended to uncover the next generation of scientists and astronauts.

For the UAE, it is crucial to find the most talented youth and ensure they have pathways to help the space sector grow. Helping Emiratis and other Arabs succeed and participate in important research and missions will help to inspire others. While the country has long invested in the infrastructure and facilities needed for a thriving aerospace sector, investing in people is just as important.[141]

With an ever-increasing number of programs and pathways, every Arab who dreams of space and wants to work in the field can have the opportunity. By increasing participation in STEM subjects and increasing the pool of potential talent, the UAE's space program will continue to grow and become a cornerstone of the knowledge economy. [142]

The UAE encourages a space culture among young Emiratis, drawing upon the historical connection of the Arab world with the skies and astronomy. Cultivating this and embedding it in the national culture will generate interest in entering the industry.

## Space Culture

Arabs have long since looked to the stars, using them to navigate the deserts and understand the changing patterns of weather. Part of the UAE's space program includes rediscovering this age-old

---

[141] Ford, Georgina, *UAE Space Agency's Arab Space Pioneers Program Trains Region's Brightest Scientific Talent*, *The Aviator*, October 1, 2021, https://www.theaviatorme.com/news/uae-space-agencys-arab-space-pioneers-program-trains-regions-brightest-scientific-talent

[142] Saikali, 2022

connection and creating a modern space culture where people talk about space and see it as an immutable part of their identity. Raising awareness of space does not just involve scientific endeavor but includes looking at its place in the wider context of art and culture.

Now, Emirati artists are recreating images taken of the cosmos and the stars are becoming the subject of stories and poems. One example of this is astrophotography, while other artists are tackling the topic of space across many mediums.

## Stargazing and Astrophotography in the UAE

As a growing hotspot for tourism, stargazing and astrophotography are increasingly important ways of showing the wonders of the cosmos. Due to its clear skies, the UAE's deserts are becoming hotspots for stargazing and perhaps draw upon the ancient local traditions of navigating by the stars and understanding the constellations.

A number of places in the UAE are contributing to the growth in stargazing, such as desert and mountain tours and events held at observatories. As an example, Al Sadeem Astronomy attracts people from across the UAE to view the sky through its telescopes. Al Thuraya Astronomy Centre and the Sharjah Centre for Astronomy and Space Sciences are excellent alternatives.[143]

An increasing number of people in the UAE are taking part in astrophotography and buying telescopes, cameras, and the other

---

[143] Duncan, Gillian, Seven of the UAE's best stargazing spots, *The National,* October 28, 2020, https://www.thenationalnews.com/uae/science/seven-of-the-uae-s-best-stargazing-spots-1.1100989

equipment needed to capture images of meteors and other striking phenomena. They are signing up for photography training courses and setting up groups to explore the country's deserts, islands, and other remote areas with low light pollution for the ultimate photograph.[144]

## Museums and Social Media

Many countries with space programs often set up museums and street art alongside education and outreach that sets space exploration as an important part of culture. Museums and educational programs in schools can help to stir interest in the space program and help locals reconnect with their cultural tapestry.

To help publicize the UAE's space program, various events and activities continue to promote the sector while a National Geographic documentary, 'Reach for the Stars' covered the UAE's space program. Documentaries and news items all help publicize the nation's achievements and ensure it is a topic of conversation.[145]

One artist even developed a stuffed toy mascot, Suhail, that accompanied Hazza Al Mansouri on his mission and is intended to attract the attention of Arab children and inspire them to see space as something attainable. Saeed Al Emadi, the artist who works at

---

[144] Sarwat, Nasir, How space culture is growing in the UAE through art and astrophotography, *The National,* September 21, 2021, https://www.thenationalnews.com/uae/2021/09/21/how-space-culture-is-growing-in-the-uae-through-art-and-astrophotography/

[145] Nasir, Sarwat, How space culture is growing in the UAE through art and astrophotography, *The National,* September 21, 2021, https://www.thenationalnews.com/uae/2021/09/21/how-space-culture-is-growing-in-the-uae-through-art-and-astrophotography/

MBRSC, believes that this is a way to interact and connect with younger audiences, starting with a social media poll to choose the mascot's name. He intends to develop the character further and give it a unique personality. Al Emadi also developed the 'Zayed's Ambition' mission patch, working with the Federal Youth Authority. [146]

MBRSC launched the Emirates Space Art Programme (ESAP) to capture the story of the UAE's space program through collaborations with artists and Jsoor, a social enterprise. This will use the country's creative industry to generate extra awareness for the space program, reaching a wider audience and telling the story. In this respect, the space program can also inspire artists in the country, helping to promote that sector while maintaining interest in the space program. [147]

For the Mars mission, the UAE set up billboards commemorating the event and commissioned street art in prominent locations. The MBRSC communications team also leverages social media by publishing striking images of the heavens.

These artistic initiatives do appear to be having an effect and more and more students are signing up for degrees in space-related STEM subjects. Many want to specialize, not just in engineering, but

---

[146] Nasir, Sarwat, Emirati artist designs a stuffed toy that flew to outer space, January 4, 2021, https://www.thenationalnews.com/uae/science/emirati-artist-designs-a-stuffed-toy-that-flew-to-outer-space-1.1139589

[147] Sircar, Nandini, UAE's milestone space explorations to come alive with art, *Khaleej Times,* September 22, 2021, https://www.khaleejtimes.com/uae/uaes-milestone-space-explorations-to-come-alive-with-art

subjects such as astrophysics and cosmology, and new courses offering practical experience in aerospace technology.

## Majarat Magazine

MBRSC launched this magazine to promote awareness of the UAE's space program and contribute to the space culture. The magazine focuses on space science and technologies, setting out to raise awareness in the UAE. It promotes the work of the MBRSC, in Arabic and English, and aims to discuss complex topics inaccessible, non-technical language. The magazine is distributed around government departments, universities, and youth clubs, as well as online.[148,149]

## Innovation and Building for the Future

The UAE actively seeks to adopt new technologies and ensure that the country's air industry and space programs remain at the forefront. Its airlines are focused on exploring how new technologies and data can help to improve efficiency and make things easier for their customers. Some of the technologies include AI, better use of data, robotics, and training simulation.

## Machine Learning and Data Democratization

Emirates is implementing machine learning to better analyze data, promote cost efficiency, and improve customer service. The country's airlines are developing data democratization programs to

---

[148] MBRSC launches new magazine to spread knowledge of space science, *WAM,* August 16, 2015, https://wam.ae/en/details/1395284377876

[149] Mohammed bin Rashid Space Centre launches magazine, *The National,*

ensure they can respond to customer demands more quickly and efficiently. With this process, everyone within an organization can assess data easily and make better decisions, improving performance and customer satisfaction.

The organization understands it needs to innovate in such a competitive aviation market. Emirates set out its objectives, which involved implementing data-driven approaches across the entire enterprise. The company set up a Center of Excellence and developed a centralized Data Lake that maintains and stores all data in one place. The company can analyze, understand, and present data to all departments.

With the ability to use data to streamline processes, the company can become more efficient, reduce waste, and maximize profitability while lowering costs. The data democratization also underpins the use of Artificial Intelligence, and the company developed teams with specialists covering a wide range of skills. [150]

Emirates is presently working with a German company to develop the Emirates AI Assistant intended to enhance the customer flight experience. It will support customers before, during, and after the flight. In the same vein, a US company will develop AI-based supply and procurement while a British tech company will develop a crew duty system.

With this technology, the UAE is making a statement of intent that it will remain at the forefront of aviation technology and

---

[150] Democratizing Data Science in an Airline – How Emirates Does It, *Hyperight,* June 2022, https://hyperight.com/democratizing-data-science-in-an-airline-how-emirates-does-it/

continue to operate some of the most advanced and efficient airlines in the world. The country will remain committed to investing in aviation technology and overcome challenges. [151]

## New Training Simulators

Emirates has installed new simulators for Boeing and Airbus in a new facility. Costing $135 million, the six simulators will over full flight simulation for Airbus A350 and Boeing 777X aircraft. Located in a purpose-built facility, the simulators, due to come online in early 2024, will increase Emirates' pilot training capability by over 50%.

The simulators are part of the new pilot training center as Emirates prepares for a new intake of pilots in 2024. With cutting edge simulation using solar power, the center joins the Emirates Flight Training Academy for cadets, Emirates Aviation University, Emirates Cabin Crew Training Centre, and other training programs for employees across the enterprise. [152]

## Biometrics and Digital Innovation

Emirates has implemented biometric check ins to speed up and improve customer service alongside a raft of other innovations. In 2019, Emirates started looking at biometric technology within its airports, especially check-in, customer lounges, and some boarding

---

[151] Bridge, Sam, Emirates says working on AI-powered flight 'assistant', May 8, 2019, https://www.arabianbusiness.com/industries/travel-hospitality/419594-emirates-says-working-on-ai-powered-flight-assistant

[152] Emirates announces massive new $135m pilot training centre in Dubai, *Arabian News,* Feb 20, 2023, https://www.arabianbusiness.com/industries/transport/dubais-emirates-to-open-135mn-pilot-training-centre

gates. Many customers have used the secure and contactless verification, especially after the pandemic.

Another Emirates innovation is self-service check in intended to speed up the customer service experience. Customers can check-in, drop off bags and, most importantly, avoid prolonged queues. In 2021, Emirates expanded the system and also implemented new systems for reporting lost/damaged baggage.[153]

## Multilingual Check In Robots

Emirates will be the first airline to use robotics to offer personalized customer services. These multilingual robots help speed up check in and lower queuing time as part of the airline's drive to use technology to improve processes and increase customer satisfaction.

Emirates is the first airline to complete the entire check-in process with robots, and they will prove especially useful for customers during flight disruptions. Future iterations will look at operations such as liaising with immigration departments and even booking hotels.

With its investment in biometrics, AI, and robots, the airline intends to make itself better able to deal with the growth in passenger numbers and free up staff for other important roles. Robots may also see use in other areas such as logistics warehouses and engineering.[154]

---

[153] Emirates accelerates digital innovation for passengers, *International Airport Review*, September 13, 2012, https://www.internationalairportreview.com/news/163755/emirates-accelerates-digital-innovation-for-passengers

[154] Kamel, Deena, Emirates airline to introduce multilingual check-in robots to cut travel time, *The National*, March 29, 2023,

## VR and the Metaverse

Emirates has embraced Virtual Reality, the Metaverse, and similar technologies to enhance customer experiences, and has converted the EXPO 2020 site into a hub for innovation and sharing new technologies. The airline is partnering with companies to deliver Virtual Reality services, allowing customers to explore its aircraft interiors before checking in to book a seat. [155]

## Supporting the UAE's Shift to a High-Tech Economy

Overall, these innovations support the UAE's adoption of a digital economy that improves the environment for businesses and for consumers. The country has used its airlines and aerospace programs to help it develop a knowledge economy, but it needs to keep innovating or find itself overtaken by other countries in the region.

## Always Think of the Future

In a few short decades, the UAE has developed at a breakneck pace, using its fossil fuel wealth to build infrastructure and educate its population. Importantly, the country's leaders did not throw money around without making sure they understood how it would help them achieve their overall vision. Every program they undertook carefully considers the future and how they will get there.

---

https://www.thenationalnews.com/business/aviation/2023/03/09/emirates-to-introduce-multilingual-check-in-robots-to-cut-travel-time/

[155] Emirates to launch NFTs and experiences in the metaverse, *Emirates,* April 14, 2022, https://www.emirates.com/media-centre/emirates-to-launch-nfts-and-experiences-in-the-metaverse/

When the UAE started investing in airlines, it also understood that it would need the infrastructure to support their growth. When they developed the space program, they knew that they would need talented and passionate employees who believed in the program. Rather than becoming vanity projects, they were investments that would deliver the country's vision of becoming a technological hub.

This willingness to think of the future remains and the UAE always looks to be a first adopter of new technologies. Just as importantly, the country's leaders understand that they will need a pool of qualified people able to implement and use them, and is investing heavily in education and training. This lies at the core of a knowledge economy and the wider plans of creating technology hubs and best-in-class facilities in the MENA region.

The fact that the UAE does not only think what it needs now, but looks at what it will need decades into the future has brought it to this point. With a raft of new innovations and young leaders and entrepreneurs who are tech-savvy, this is set to continue long into the future, whether the UAE develops spaceports, sends people to Mars, or continues to grow as a major aviation and airport hub.

# CHAPTER 9

## LEADERSHIP LESSONS FROM THE UAE'S AVIATION AND SPACE JOURNEY

The UAE's journey in aviation and space demonstrates the power of effective leadership. From the visionary leadership of the UAE leadership to the perseverance of the first UAE astronauts, there are many leadership lessons to be learned from the country's journey.

## The Vison

The UAE aviation industry and space industry all stemmed from a vision for the future, of setting up a national airline, which the country achieved and is now a global leader. With the space program, the UAE is setting additional long-term goals to work towards, such as initiating the Mars 2117 program to develop technology with a vision spanning decades in mind. The country's leaders had a strong idea of what they wanted the country to work towards and understood that they needed to shift from a fossil-fuel based economy to a modern, mixed model.

This idea of having a vision pervades through every part of the country, and the leaders of its airlines and aerospace industry always seem to understand the destination. Every action they take is focused on this and ensures that every policy and every investment move them a little closer to the final destination. The vision is not an esoteric concept discussed only by leaders, but a tangible future shared with the population and the rest of the world.

The UAE has been very open in communicating its vision and this helps the population buy-in to the idea. Private enterprises are more willing to take risks and invest if they know that the aerospace industry is here for the long haul and that they will receive support. Young Emiratis, now aware that it is possible to build a career in the science and technology sector, or even become a pilot or astronaut, can safely study STEM subjects knowing that they will find work when they graduate.

## Building Partnerships

Throughout the process, from setting up the airline to developing the space program, the UAE realized the importance of building partnerships with companies and institutions. From the start, the partnership with Pakistan International Airlines helped Emirates through the complex process of setting up an airline. The country has been proactive in building partnerships with aircraft manufacturers and other organizations. This taps into their expertise and helps to build a strong knowledge base in the country.

In the same way, the UAE understands that it needs private sector involvement and innovation as part of the space program, with programs such as Hub 71. With initiatives intended to use local suppliers and businesses for its developing economy, this creates strong partnerships with the private sector and helps to keep investment circling in the local economy.[156]

---

[156] Cresniov, Alex, As UAE's space sector grows in stature, SpaceTech fund and accelerator are natural next steps, *Arabian Business,* March 24, 2022, https://www.arabianbusiness.com/opinion/as-uaes-space-sector-grows-in-stature-spacetech-fund-and-accelerator-are-natural-next-steps

Many other countries have space programs stretching back decades, so the UAE Space Agency patiently established partnerships with NASA, the ESA, and Roscosmos. It also collaborates with Japan, China, and other organizations to train its astronauts, open up the possibility of manned missions, and launch satellites. All of these are raising the profile of the country's growing space industry and ensuring that it can continue to develop and initiate its own programs.

## Find the Best People

While the UAE actively seeks to develop national expertise and train and educate its own citizens for influential roles, the leaders understood the importance of finding experienced people from elsewhere when needed. For example, Emirates hired Maurice Flanagan and later Tim Clark, which brought years of ability and proven track records that set the company on the right path from the start. While the UAE does want to prioritize local talent, its leaders are aware of the need for importing expertise when needed.

As an example of how the UAE searches for the best people, during its astronaut training program, the UAE Space Agency set up stringent testing and selection. This process had the end goal of making sure that it sent the best candidates to final selection with Roscosmos and NASA. Not only are its astronauts motivated and highly capable, but they are great communicators with a passion for sharing their experiences in the UAE and across the Arab world. In turn, this will inspire future generations and ensure that the program continues to attract strong candidates.

One area in which the UAE is strong is ensuring that gender plays no role in attracting the right candidates. Female Emiratis see women on astronaut training courses, managing important programs, and taking positions as ministers, with no barriers to success based on gender. By promoting women in the workplace and encouraging them to pursue careers in science and technology, the UAE makes sure that the best people always have an opportunity to shine.

## Brand Awareness

Brand awareness is a huge part of the UAE's growth because it has to operate in highly competitive marketplaces. For example, airlines operate in one of the most cut-throat environments with very thin profit margins. Accordingly, Emirates invests a lot of resources in publicity and marketing to increase the recognizability of its brand. The airline marketed its brand aggressively and looked for sectors with growth potential and high international visibility, like the English Premier League.

However, marketing must be supported, especially for a company, like Emirates, that operates at the higher end of the market. It has to offer very high-quality service and reliable flights, and its customers like to see new technologies and approaches that give a unique customer experience. Reputation is everything and any erosion of quality will render the branding less effective.

Branding does not just cover companies and the UAE now promotes itself through tourism and marketing. Abu Dhabi and Dubai enjoy great international reputations and the country wants to maintain this. Building a high technology economy means developing trust so that partners and investors know that they will reap rewards and be treated fairly.

## Philanthropy

Emirates always followed a philosophy of supporting causes, partly because it is simply the right thing to do and partly because it builds trust in the brand. As an example with the Emirates Airline Foundation.

Over the years, the UAE has actively encouraged private and public philanthropy, supporting charities and initiatives worldwide and always being one of the first countries to offer humanitarian aid. The country is now recognized as a hub for philanthropy and supporting the poorest members of its society.[157,158]

Domestically, this strengthens the social contract between leaders and people and shows that the vision for the future also includes them. Internationally, philanthropy builds strong relationships between nations and goes some way to combating rising tensions in the world. It also helps when trying to build partnerships with other nations, institutions, and large commercial enterprises.

Donations from government and individuals, whether financial or in terms of time and mentoring, further improve society and help the country's economy. Support for education, helping people with

---

[157] Ahmen, Maram, Opinion: The UAE's philanthropy boom, *Devex*, April 9, 2019, https://www.devex.com/news/opinion-the-uae-s-philanthropy-boom-94642

[158] The United Arab Emirates: Philanthropy Law Report, *International Center for Not-for-Profit Law*, 2023, https://www.icnl.org/wp-content/uploads/UAE-Philanthropy-Law-Report-May-2023.pdf

scholarships, and helping businesses can develop a skilled workforce and also make sure that the potential scientists, astronauts, and leaders of the future have opportunities. Apart from being morally right, philanthropy by an organization can deliver long term benefits and mutual goodwill.[159]

## Quality

Emirates is consistently voted one of the world's top airlines, and its focus on quality and customer service has been a major factor in its growth. National airlines can be a powerful way of projecting the image of a country, and a strong reputation for innovation, excellent service, reliability, and unique customer experiences can build positive perceptions of the UAE.

In the same way, the many hotels and other tourism-related businesses can further enhance the image of the country as a safe and clean destination. Behind the scenes, the UAE's efficient logistics centers and growing industrial base further enhances the reputation of the country for quality. The country is trying to establish itself as an international hub and attract hi-tech companies and manufacturing where quality is of paramount importance.

For any organization, maintaining high quality means pursuing excellence and making sure that it meets the needs and expectations of customers, investors, and potential partners. The UAE emphasizes this and seeks to embed it in all of its institutions, commercial sectors,

---

[159] Johnson, Paula D. and Rafim, Tauriq, Great Expectations The Growth of Institutional Philanthropy in the United Arab Emirates, *Belfer Center,* April 2018, https://www.belfercenter.org/sites/default/files/files/publication/Growth-of-Institutional-Philanthropy-UAE-Harvard-Report_web.pdf

and education system to help it maintain its branding and reputation, as well as moving the country closer to its visions for the future.

## Willingness to Embrace New Technology

For a country seeking to diversify and develop a knowledge-based economy, embracing new technologies and innovations throughout the economy is crucial. In an increasingly competitive world, failing to innovate can see a country struggle as investors seek other options. On the other hand, opening up to new technology can develop a reputation for cultivating innovation and supporting businesses and entrepreneurs with ideas.

The UAE has established centers of innovation, developed research centers and fostered strong academic institutions to help forge partnerships with global organizations. For example, using new technologies has always driven success for Emirates and the space program. Using machine learning and state-of-the-art simulators for pilot training keep Emirates ahead of the competition.[160]

This focus on new technologies and modern infrastructure means that the UAE can attract foreign direct investment and expertise. Aviation and the space programs are two important areas where innovation drives economic growth and builds a reputation. By remaining at the forefront of technological advancement and starting to develop their own technologies as well as importing foreign options, they are building foundations for the future.

---

[160] Emirates announces massive new $135m pilot training centre in Dubai, *Arabian News,* Feb 20, 2023, https://www.arabianbusiness.com/industries/transport/dubais-emirates-to-open-135mn-pilot-training-centre

The country's investment in education and its people encourages innovation and creativity, helping the nation grow its economy and move closer to achieving its visions. For any organization, investing in education, research, and innovation is a way to safeguard the future and create a culture of success.

# CHAPTER 10

## CONCLUSION

In conclusion, the UAE's incredible space and aviation journey is a monument to the nation's clear vision and its leadership's unrelenting dedication to fostering positive change. A dream to upgrade and advance the country into the aerospace industry was started from the UAE's founding. Sheikh Zayed bin Sultan Al Nahyan, whose forward-thinking futuristic objectives included sending Emiratis into the unexplored reaches of the aerospace and space frontier, served as the foundation for this dream.

The UAE views space as more than just a place for scientific research. It advocates for space rules to preserve space as a haven for peaceful purposes. It sees space as a means of fostering international cooperation and diplomacy. This pursuit is a clear manifestation of the UAE's aspiration to make a positive impact on the world stage.

Furthermore, the UAE's strategic investments in aviation and space constitute an integral part of its overarching plan to diversify its economy and steer away from the dependency on fossil fuels. The nation is actively fostering a knowledge-based economy as it goes through this transformation, with aerospace emerging as a crucial industry for expansion and advancement. In addition to helping the country diversify economically, the space sector and its aspirational goals enhance the United Arab Emirates' reputation as a center for cutting-edge research in the Middle East and beyond.

Naturally, reaching these objectives will require making ongoing large infrastructural investments, forming alliances with foreign organizations, and developing the country's human resources. The UAE's continued focus on these important areas demonstrates its determination to remain a hub for scientific advancement now and into the future for space technology as well as the larger aerospace industry.

The leadership lessons and key takeaways from this book which I hereby submit humbly, I do hope have inspired you to apply in your everyday life to experience the same out-of-this-world success are herein included as your guide:

1.  **The Importance of Vision and Long-Term Goals:**

    -   Start with a clear, compelling **vision** for the future.
    -   Align the organization's mission with long-term objectives.
    -   Foster a sense of **purpose** that transcends short-term gains.

2.  **Be Proactive and Build the Foundations with the End in Mind:**

    -   Anticipate challenges and act proactively.
    -   Set a course for the future while maintaining a focus on present actions.
    -   Lay the groundwork for success through strategic planning and **building partnerships**.

3.  **Focus on the Most Important Tasks to Support Growth:**

    -   Identify and prioritize critical tasks that drive growth.
    -   Allocate resources efficiently to support key initiatives.

- Maintain a results-oriented approach that bolsters the organization's expansion and enhances **brand awareness**.

4. **Collaborate and Look for Win-Win Collaboration:**

- Cultivate a culture of collaboration and open communication.
- Seek mutually beneficial partnerships that elevate all involved parties.
- Harness the power of teamwork and shared goals for sustainable success and effective **philanthropy**.

5. **Synergize and Integrate Resources:**

- Recognize the potential in combining diverse talents and resources.
- Promote integration and cooperation among different parts of the organization.
- Create synergy to achieve outcomes greater than the sum of individual efforts and ensure **quality**.

6. **Find the Right People and Let Them Inspire Others:**

- Identify and nurture talented individuals who align with the organization's vision.
- Empower and entrust leaders to inspire and mentor others.
- Encourage a culture of leadership development and succession planning to enhance **quality** and the organization's **brand awareness**.

7. **Always Look to the Future, Always Think of the Future:**

- Embrace a forward-thinking mindset that anticipates change.
- Continuously adapt to evolving circumstances and emerging opportunities, **willingness to embrace new technology**.
- Develop a strategic agility that keeps the organization on the path to future success, reinforcing the commitment to long-term **vision**.

8. **Never Give Up, Never Surrender:**

- Embrace unwavering determination in the face of adversity.
- In the challenging and often unpredictable realm of space and aerospace, persist in the pursuit of goals and **vision**.
- Demonstrate resilience, a relentless spirit, and a commitment to overcoming obstacles, ensuring that setbacks become stepping stones toward success.

The idea of manned missions and possibly human settlement on the Red Planet has changed from being a far-off fantasy to a real objective, with the UAE standing proudly as only the fifth nation to reach the planet. The nation has already started working on developing the required technology, and with unyielding resolve, it is getting closer to realizing this stretch goal. The goal of establishing a human-populated settlement on Mars itself is an example of its unwavering commitment to advancing humanity and shows its readiness to push boundaries.

Outside of science, people are fascinated by space because of its unmistakable romantic appeal. The sense of pride that envelops Emiratis regarding their astronauts and the Mars mission resonates with people all across the world. The UAE's pioneering spirit in space exploration acts as an inspiration to other countries and individuals, serving as a reminder that everyone has the opportunity to explore and improve our planet in the limitless cosmos.

The UAE's path in aviation and space is a tribute to the power of visionary leadership, perseverance, and knowledge-seeking in the larger context of leadership. It serves as a reminder that we may achieve greatness by pursuing our goals and rising to the occasion, paving the way for advancement, collaboration, and creativity.

# NOTES

Having traveled on Emirates Airlines for 20-plus years, one of the lasting positive impacts it has made on every passenger at the end of any flight is the request to donate whatever change and in whatever denomination each traveler had on hand to the Emirates Airline Foundation. I often found myself taking out the loose change in US Dollars, UK Pounds, Euros, and the occasional Japanese Yen or Brazilian Real and placing it into the donation bag the Emirates Crew would pass around the cabin.

The Emirates Airline Foundation is a non-profit charity organization which aims to improve the quality of life for children, regardless of geographical, political, or religious boundaries, and to help them maintain or improve their human dignity.

A portion of the proceeds from sales of this book will be donated to the Emirates Airline Foundation. I encourage you to donate next time you are on an Emirates flight or to donate directly on their website.

Thank you.